SCIENCE OF MIND
STUDY COURSE

Twelve Lessons
to Achieve Peace of Mind

by

Dr. Frederick Bailes

THE BOOK TREE
San Diego, California

First Published 1951
Dr. Frederick Bailes

© 1951
Dr. Frederick Bailes

ISBN 978-1-58509-387-8

cover photo
© Paul Tice

Cover layout
Paul Tice

Published by
The Book Tree
San Diego, CA 92176
www.thebooktree.com

We provide fascinating and educational products to help awaken the public to new ideas
and information that would not be available otherwise.
Call 1 (800) 700-8733 for our FREE BOOK TREE CATALOG.

SCIENCE OF MIND

Home-Study Extension Course

(copyright 1951)

by

DR. FREDERICK BAILES

CONTENTS

SCIENCE OF MIND

Home-Study Extension Course

(copyright 1951)

by

DR. FREDERICK BAILES

INTRODUCTION

THIS CHANGING WORLD

Today, the world stands at the crossroads of civilization. It must move in one of two directions—either backward to devastating carnage and ultimate barbarism or forward toward spiritual understanding and the highest civilization ever seen on this earth. The direction it takes is not foreordained; it is not determined by blind Fate. Man is free to go in whichever direction he chooses.

KEY TO PEACE

The students of this philosophy may well decide humanity's destiny. Starting your inquiry into the universal forces, which may be used for good or ill, you are being given a key to the future—a key which may be used to bring man out of his prison of materialism and violence into the bright light of his highest fulfillment, or which may be used to lock, with dread finality, the door that seals him into a self-chosen doom.

A FAST-GROWING MOVEMENT

The issues are delicately balanced. The forces of materialism are noisy; they get the headlines; therefore those who are influenced by the sensational think the worst is inevitable. But beneath the surface of headlined events is a movement comparable to the build-up of a great ground swell. This movement is the silent power of man's inner spiritual self.

Not organized or articulate, it has not yet been noticed by the politicians whose ears hear only the sounds of self-seeking voting blocs. It is scorned by the advocates of force who are familiar only with the power of explosives. And it has not yet been recognized by millions of timorous souls who, understanding little of world affairs, shrink in terror at the grim possibilities of world-destruction.

A WORLD MOVEMENT

This resistless movement is not confined to any one religious group, for men of all groups are part of it. It is not localized in this country, for it is the voice of God in all humanity. Across our desk come daily reports indicating the widespread nature of this inner spiritual movement which, we believe, will save humanity and civilization.

From Japan is sent this word: "There are 85,000 members of our group studying and working for peace."

From Austria: "Please send teachers. Our people are ready for this knowledge."

From Czechoslovakia: "We are groping toward what we feel to be the ultimate solution to this problem of peace in a changing world."

From Germany: "600,000 are members of this brotherhood seeking true foundations for peace of mind and body."

From Belgium, Italy, France, India, and the British Isles come letters asking for written instruction or teachers who can rapidly lead the people into a knowledge of their inherent, God-given power to control destructive forces now loose in the world. Those whom we have sent abroad to answer this call report an enthusiastic eagerness on the part of their listeners to walk this inner path—the path of man's union with the Infinite. They also tell of the astoundingly beneficial results obtained by those who have followed this new understanding of spiritual force.

Therefore, we congratulate you on your decision to become one of that invisible brotherhood of those who are joined in spirit throughout the world. Not only should you manifest the fulfillment of your personal desires, but you have become one of those whose thought-patterns are even now remaking the world.

SOME PRELIMINARY INSTRUCTIONS

To you, the student of this course, who are now a part of this, the greatest dynamic on earth, we say, "Don't work at your studies tensely with a straining for results, for 'It is not by might, nor by power, but by my Spirit, saith the Lord'." (Zech. 4:6.) Just let the silent power of the Infinite Healing Presence flow through you. When we use the term "Infinite Healing Presence," we mean that indwelling Wisdom of the ages, which holds the stars in their courses and the atoms in a rock, that heals a cut finger, cements a broken bone, and that impels the tree roots to seek water. Difficult to describe, its activity has been noted by the observant throughout the ages. For want of a better name, men have called it God, the superintending and sustaining Intelligence of the universe.

WHERE POWER LIES

At the outset of your studies, please make sure that you understand the FUNDAMENTAL PRINCIPLE that YOU do not create power. You merely lay hold on that Invisible Power which has always existed. Heretofore, you may have been unaware of it. Now, aware of it, you learn how to align yourself with it, and IT does the work.

POWER WITHIN YOU

Moreover, cultivate the conviction that man needs NOTHING outside of himself. Already within him is the Infinite Healing Intelligence, waiting to go to work. As the lessons progress, you will learn the various approaches to this Power and how to apply the principle to specific areas of action.

NEED FOR OPEN-MINDEDNESS

It is imperative that the student be OPEN-MINDED. Truth never changes, but our understanding of it does. Newer views are sometimes in conflict with older theology, but they are not dangerous because of this. God is still God, no matter how He is described. Faith is still faith, even when expressed in scientific and modern terminology, rather than in orthodox or archaic language.

DEVELOPING GOD-CONSCIOUSNESS

The earth consciousness must be changed to a God-consciousness, which carries in Itself all fulfillment. This is not realized by mastering a succession of facts. It comes through a changed FEELING, a changed belief which finally becomes a warm inward conviction. This latter is what is called KNOWING THE TRUTH.

PRACTICE IS ESSENTIAL

We must also put our lessons into practice. Without a wholehearted willingness to follow the truth wherever it may lead, there can be no change in our affairs. Truth never becomes OUR OWN until we apply it.

LIKE ATTRACTS LIKE

We can begin, at this moment, to apply Truth by facing our own responsibility for what has happened to us. We can say something like this: "WHATEVER SITUATION I AM IN TODAY IS THE DIRECT RESULT OF MY PAST THINKING. I am exactly where I belong by right of consciousness. True, the perfidy of others or their failure to co-operate may have contributed to my misfortune; but the accident which seemed NOT to have been my fault, or the illness which seemed NOT to come through any fault of mine was made possible by the general tendency of my thought. This, in some way, attracted to me these persons, events, or things which have happened to me, even while I was longing for, praying for, and trying to get their very opposites."

INTELLECTUAL HONESTY REQUIRED

The key to man's freedom is his thought. If we can be courageous enough to admit that the unfortunate experiences in our lives have, in some way, been attracted by our thinking, we have laid the foundation for their removal through a change in our thought. But if our pride or our stubbornness keeps us from admitting the first, we thereby set in motion a law that prevents the second from bringing our deliverance.

SET DEFINITE STUDY PERIOD

Upon receipt of the lessons, we strongly suggest that you set aside a definite time each week, for the next twelve weeks, in which you will start the study of each new lesson and the reading of recommended books on the subject. Read, then thoughtfully reread the new lesson to absorb the underlying principal thoughts deeply into your consciousness. The success of this course for you lies in your CHANGING A CONSCIOUSNESS which has brought you things you do not like into one which brings you your most cherished desires.

QUESTIONS MAY ANSWER THEMSELVES

Questions will come to your mind from time to time as you proceed through the course. This is well, for it indicates growth. We recommend that you set aside a portion of your notebook to record them, BUT DO NOT WRITE US FOR THE ANSWERS YET. Our many years of teaching many thousands of students have shown us how to anticipate your questions. We have woven the answers through the course at a time when the student is best prepared with background to grasp them.

As you master the lessons, especially the last six, you will be able to go through your notebook and check off many questions which puzzled you during the early lessons.

If, at the END of the course, you still have points which have not been made clear, and which BEAR DIRECTLY UPON THIS TEACHING, we shall be very happy to answer them for you.

gives it beautiful, constructive thoughts, it is his friend, who fabricates for him, in the depths of his inner world, that which is beautiful and constructive in his outer world. If his thoughts are otherwise, the result will be otherwise; for the loom of mind "does unto us as we believe."

Life never lets us down; we let ourselves down. Life never fails us; we fail it. Life is a part of Cause and Effect; Cause and Effect is likewise part of Life, the greatest ally one could ever have. But we've so filled our thought with the gloomy, the destructive, that we have failed to give the loom the sort of materials with which it could weave a good pattern.

By now, it must be apparent to the student that, while man's mind is one and indivisible, it has two interacting phases, which, for the purpose of study, we take up separately. And if we seem repetitious, it is because our thirty years' teaching of this subject have revealed that those students succeed best who learn clearly to separate the activities and characteristics of the two levels of mind.

SURFACE (CONSCIOUS) MIND HAS POWER TO CHOOSE

SURFACE mind is that which we use when getting a telephone number. We consciously think of each digit before dialing it. When one learns to play the piano, also, SURFACE mind consciously directs the playing of each note through repetition until one has become so familiar with piano technique that individual finger movements have passed into DEEPER mind, leaving the surface phase free for reading the score and, if desired, words of a song that the performer wants to sing.

SURFACE mind is characterized by the words, "I CHOOSE."

DEEPER (SUBCONSCIOUS) MIND CARRIES OUT OUR CHOICES

DEEPER mind is habitual mind. Whatever is held often enough or vividly enough in SURFACE mind eventually passes into DEEPER mind, where it continues to act automatically. This is the process by which man learns everything that he learns.

DEEPER mind is characterized by the words, "I OBEY." It is obedient to the mandates of SURFACE mind.

SCIENCE OF MIND

Home-Study Extension Course

(copyright 1951)

by

DR. FREDERICK BAILES

LESSON I

SCIENCE OF MIND TERMINOLOGY

Certain psychological terms which tend to confuse many students are in use in explaining man's thought processes. Some of them are "objective mind," "subjective mind," "conscious mind," "unconscious mind," and "subconscious mind." Before we go any further, we shall simplify these terms and make them easy to remember.

Suppose we think of the mind as though it were an ocean. The ocean has a surface, and it has depths. Man sailing on the surface can see what floats there in the way of flotsam and jetsam. He can map the surface showing the ocean's fingers reaching into bays and inlets. He is familiar with the surface calms and with rough water whipped up by storms.

Oceanographers tell us that the stormiest weather involves only a few fathoms of the surface and that below lie the great depths, undisturbed and still, except for submarine currents which flow calmly and ceaselessly on their set courses. No one can tell where the surface ends and the depths begin, for the ocean is all one, and it is only for purposes of description that it is divided into "surface" and "depths."

MIND HAS SURFACE AND DEPTHS

The human mind likewise is all one, but because two types of activities are carried on in man's mind, we divide the spheres in which these different activities take place into two, to which are given the names SURFACE mind and DEEPER mind. The student must clearly remember that these are not two minds; they are merely two views of mind or two spheres of activity within one mind.

In the past the SURFACE mind has been called "conscious" or "objective" mind. The depths have been called "subconscious," "unconscious," or "subjective" mind. This is because man is conscious of what takes place in his SURFACE mind, but not conscious of what takes place in the depths. Also, his conscious mind produces effects through conscious choice, as when he picks up a pen and writes his name. On the other hand, without any conscious choice his heart is kept beating and the process of digestion is carried on by his subconscious mind through processes of which he is not in conscious control. Nothing goes on anywhere in the universe or within his own body without some action of mind.

The following parallel columns give a clear summary of the terms as they are used in this course:

SURFACE Mind	DEEPER Mind
Conscious Mind	Unconscious Mind
Objective Mind	Subconscious Mind
	Subjective Mind

DEEPER MIND—THE STOREHOUSE OF EXPERIENCE

A man may have a conscious experience today; tomorrow or next year he will have "forgotten" it; yet it has not gone out of existence. It has passed down from his SURFACE mind into his DEEPER mind, where it is stored for future reference. What we call memory or recollection is merely the call of the SURFACE mind for something that has been stored in the DEEPER mind. This complex and mysterious interaction of the two results in past experiences being yielded up for present use.

DEEPER MIND CREATES OUR EXPERIENCE

Every experience through which we have ever passed is thus stored away for future reference. Thought is an active thing, never still, always trying to find an outlet in some form. Each thought retains its own distinctive character and can work ONLY according to its own nature. Negative, destructive thoughts continue to work negatively beneath the surface, and in due time will yield up some outer experience which corresponds to them. We may have long forgotten the storing of the original thought and are, therefore, surprised when we find troublesome things happening to us. There is nothing mysterious or unfair about this. We are not being singled out by Fate for its buffetings. We are only reaping what we have sown, sometime, somewhere.

In like manner, every positive, constructive thought seeks to find an outlet. Nothing is ever wasted. Those for whom some kindness was done may seem unappreciative; our motives may have been questioned or misunderstood so that we regret having sacrificed some advantage in order to do the right thing. But the law of one's thought continues to operate regardless of others' reactions; and sometime, perhaps long after we have forgotten it, that kindness will yield its fruit in some windfall of happiness coming from a totally different quarter.

THOUGHTS ARE SEEDS IN THE CREATIVE SOIL OF MIND

Man is sowing seeds of thought every time he thinks. Buried beneath the soil of mind, the good and the bad seeds are indwelt by the same principle of life. They grow silently together, like the tares and the wheat, until the harvest.

Some come to harvest-time one year, some another, but eventually all man's thoughts appear in some form in his life and affairs. This will explain why we said in our Introduction that each of us, at any moment, is exactly where he belongs by right of consciousness. There is no "fate" but our sowings; there is no "destiny" but our choices; there are no "bad breaks" or "bad luck" but the silent unfolding from the DEEPER mind of that which we planted foolishly and in our ignorance.

In this course we shall learn to plant wisely, according to the true science of menticulture. An understanding of this will enable us to wipe out self-pity and complaint, for it places squarely on our own doorstep both the causes of our unhappiness and the beginning of our happiness. Moreover, it removes the seething resentments which poison the lives of many persons, because it makes plain that others could never have hurt us unless we first had prepared the soil and planted the seeds. Naturally they are culpable because of their unkindness, but the circling Law of Cause and Effect will quite impersonally bring into their lives the results of their own choices. This is why a wise student of mind once said, "Dearly beloved, avenge not yourselves. . . . Vengeance is mine; I will repay . . . saith the Lord." (Rom. 12:19)

"LORD" IN BIBLE IS "LAW" IN SCIENCE OF MIND

Here it might be well to point out that the Bible is made more understandable and reasonable when one understands a certain principle of interpretation, which is this: the word "Law" can usually be substituted for "Lord." God is not vengeful, but the impersonal Law of Cause and Effect produces what looks like vengeance. It is not done with punitive intent, however, any more than the river punishes with drowning the person who falls into it before he has learned to swim. The river will drown him without hating him. On the other hand, if he has learned how to swim, it will, without loving him, buoy him up as he makes for the shore. In both cases it is utterly impersonal.

THE PROBLEM OF EVIL

The Law of Cause and Effect is equally impersonal. It will produce illness or health, poverty or plenty, happiness or unhappiness, with the same completeness. Thus, when the Bible says in effect, "I am the Lord; I create good and I create evil," (Isa. 45:7) those who have not understood the interchangeability of "Lord" and "Law" have said, "How can it be that a God of love creates evil also?" The answer is that the Law (Lord) is the automatic bringer of man's thought into form. If man's thought is evil, "I the Law" create it into evil. If his thought is good, "I the Law" create it into good. This is the universal Law of CAUSE AND EFFECT, which is the only way in which God, the Infinite Intelligence, works.

DEEPER MIND IS LIKE A LOOM

Perhaps an illustration would be apt at this point. We all know enough about the principles of rug-weaving to know that there are a loom, threads, a rug, and a weaver. The loom has only one task: that is, to keep weaving. It does not decide whether it will weave a beautiful or an ugly rug; hour after hour it moves back and forth, while yard after yard of rug comes slowly forth at the other end of the loom.

The weaver watching it may be displeased and outraged by what he sees coming out, but he does not berate the loom and say, "Why have you done this to me?" He does not sit at the other end crying over the ugly pattern, wishing it would somehow change into a thing of beauty. He knows that the only place where beauty can be made to replace ugliness is on the rack of spools at the other end BEFORE the weaving apparatus gets it, and so he goes to that end and changes the threads. He takes off a dark spool, replacing it with a brighter color; he exchanges a gaudy purple for a mellow gold. Then he starts the machine once more, and as he watches what NOW comes out at the other end, he is pleased.

The loom, however, doesn't care. It is impersonal. It has no choice but to weave whatever threads are given it, and it does so according to the pattern set by the weaver. The weaver is responsible for the result.

Daily, man's loom of mind weaves the pattern of his life. If he does not like the pattern, he is foolish to sit crying about it or wishing it would change. He is wrong to complain about "luck," or to berate "Providence." He, and he alone, is the weaver. Using intelligence, he must alter his threads of thought by changing his harsh, critical attitudes for more kindly, tolerant ones. He must cease his hidden hostilities; he must stop thinking that the world is against him. He must remove from his mind the ugly green of envy and grudges, the dingy black of pessimism. He must banish thoughts of lack and limitation, replacing them with the expectancy of good. He must replace his morbid thoughts about the illnesses of man with a quiet assurance of the Infinite Healing Presence within. All these and many more thought-patterns we shall discuss as the course progresses.

THE UNIVERSE IS FAIR

In the beginning, we want the student to gain the conviction that his DEEPER mind is the loom which momentarily weaves the threads of his thought into the stuff of his outer world, and that the loom is always completely dependable, never dropping a thread of thought, but ceaselessly weaving what he gives. Just so long as he

- 5 -

gives it beautiful, constructive thoughts, it is his friend, who fabricates for him, in the depths of his inner world, that which is beautiful and constructive in his outer world. If his thoughts are otherwise, the result will be otherwise; for the loom of mind "does unto us as we believe."

Life never lets us down; we let ourselves down. Life never fails us; we fail it. Life is a part of Cause and Effect; Cause and Effect is likewise part of Life, the greatest ally one could ever have. But we've so filled our thought with the gloomy, the destructive, that we have failed to give the loom the sort of materials with which it could weave a good pattern.

By now, it must be apparent to the student that, while man's mind is one and indivisible, it has two interacting phases, which, for the purpose of study, we take up separately. And if we seem repetitious, it is because our thirty years' teaching of this subject have revealed that those students succeed best who learn clearly to separate the activities and characteristics of the two levels of mind.

SURFACE (CONSCIOUS) MIND HAS POWER TO CHOOSE

SURFACE mind is that which we use when getting a telephone number. We consciously think of each digit before dialing it. When one learns to play the piano, also, SURFACE mind consciously directs the playing of each note through repetition until one has become so familiar with piano technique that individual finger movements have passed into DEEPER mind, leaving the surface phase free for reading the score and, if desired, words of a song that the performer wants to sing.

SURFACE mind is characterized by the words, "I CHOOSE."

DEEPER (SUBCONSCIOUS) MIND CARRIES OUT OUR CHOICES

DEEPER mind is habitual mind. Whatever is held often enough or vividly enough in SURFACE mind eventually passes into DEEPER mind, where it continues to act automatically. This is the process by which man learns everything that he learns.

DEEPER mind is characterized by the words, "I OBEY." It is obedient to the mandates of SURFACE mind.

A negative disposition, for instance, is the result of repeated negative thoughts which have sunk into DEEPER mind and which have now become habitual. But a cheerful, happy disposition may become just as automatic by conscious repetition of positive thoughts. Thus it is not true that some are blessed with positive natures, and others cursed with the opposite. People are not born optimists or pessimists; they learn to be what they are. That which anyone earnestly desires to be, he may become, not, however, by waving a magic wand but by the same procedure he uses to learn to play the piano or to swim.

To sum it up, SURFACE mind is what sees, estimates, values, selects, and chooses what shall go through DEEPER mind, which takes the material given it and weaves it into the outer pattern of man's life.

THE IMPORTANCE OF CHOICE

Nothing is ever forced upon us without our consent. Every moment that we live, we are choosing something. Often our choices are made so rapidly that we are not conscious of the process of choice, but it is there, nevertheless. For example, when we say, "Three times three is nine," there are a great many lightning-like choices which come before this conclusion. We must decide that it is not six, eight, five, or some other number. A child, unfamiliar with multiplication, might hit on any other number.

We who attended school under the older system recall the deadly monotony of daily repeating in unison, "Two and two are four. Three and three are six." This was a process of training in choice, whereby we rejected the wrong answers and chose the correct one. After a time these correct answers became automatic with us, because they had dropped into DEEPER mind, which released them on demand.

Anything which is repeatedly chosen by SURFACE mind is eventually stored in DEEPER mind. Though it may sometimes be difficult to recall, DEEPER mind never forgets anything that SURFACE mind has released to it in order to focus on something else.

MAN'S DEEPER MIND IS PART OF INFINITE MIND

DEEPER mind is the fabricating or constructing Power which lies within man, but it is by no means all of that Power; it is only that part of the great Subjective Mind of the Infinite which continually streams through man. This Infinite Subjective Mind shows itself as a WISDOM manifesting not only within man but throughout the universe.

This activity of WISDOM is seen in the orderly march of the planets around the sun, in the movement of other vaster galaxies around other vaster centers, in the confluence of great currents of energy which stream from hidden centers throughout interstellar space. We see the atom to be a miniature solar system. We find a curious mathematical exactness in the structure of crystals and cells. We see a WISDOM that knows how to build a perfect human body in approximately 280 days, fully equipped to start its earthly life-cycle. Time would fail even to hint at the widespread activities of this WISDOM; but it speaks to us of some Mathematical Thinker behind the universe, and operating through the universe.

MEANING OF THE "CHRISTOS"

Observant men of all ages have noticed this hidden WISDOM. Some have called it Universal Intelligence, an impersonal name. Others have called it God, personal in a broad sense. In the SCIENCE OF MIND it is called the Infinite Healing Presence. Perhaps the most general name throughout the ages has been the *christos*, meaning WISDOM. The *christos* is not a person; it is an inner Light. It is that "Light, which lighteth every man that cometh into the world." (John 1:9.) This Light, or WISDOM, was the secret of the power of Jesus, who was wide open to it from the spiritual side. (Please take note that *christos* is a common noun, therefore not capitalized.)

This WISDOM, or *christos*, lies deep in the mental make-up of every soul born into the universe. It knows how to keep the heart beating with mathematical regularity. It heals a cut, almost as soon as the cut occurs, by a mysterious chemical process which man does not know how to duplicate. In like manner, it heals broken bones by arranging for the outpouring of a "bone-cement" which welds the broken ends together.

One of the purposes of this course, if not the chief purpose, is to study the nature of this *christos* and the ways in which man can co-operate with it for the healing of any sort of wrong action in body or environment.

In later lessons definite techniques will be presented, and the student will find that he need have no superstitious awe in approaching the *christos*, for its action is as definite and as natural as the action of electricity or of aerodynamics. When one learns correctly how to align himself with its working principles, he can draw into his life those things which he formerly thought to be accessible only to "luckier" persons.

THE "CHRISTOS"—CENTRAL DYNAMIC OF ALL TRUE RELIGIONS

While the SCIENCE OF MIND is not primarily a system of religion, it fits within the framework of any and all religions. Any religion that has ever altered men's lives, from ancient times down to our myriad Christian sects, has done it through the power of the *christos*.

This Infinite Healing Presence, or *christos*, is broader than any sectarian system, and none has any monopoly on it. Under whatever name it appears, it is the central dynamic of any worth-while religion. It is the living center around which creed, form, ritual, and ceremony are all built. The former is the heart; the latter are the trappings. The former is the fundamental without which there can be no true religion; the latter may be selected according to the preference of the individual.

Without the *christos,* any so-called religion is a mere empty bag of ethics, furnishing no dynamic which will enable the adherent to attain mastery over himself or his environment. We do not ask our students to leave their own churches; they will be better members of these for having a clearer understanding of the *christos.*

THE "CHRISTOS" IS THE POWER

All the great spiritual leaders of antiquity, as well as those of modern times, have had a deep sense of the nearness and availability of the Infinite Healing *christos.* These men would not have become great spiritual leaders had they not found this secret of power; they would have been merely advocates of a beautiful system of ethics dangled before men to tantalize them with some highly desirable ideal which they were powerless to reach. But testifying to their knowledge of the *christos* within were the "signs and wonders" that followed the work of the founders. The dead crystallization into form, ritual, and creed which settles upon all religions when they become large and outwardly powerful is due to the loss of the fresh, vivid awareness of the *christos* as the active SPIRITUAL principle of life. They become rich, respected, dignified—but dead.

JESUS—THE EMBODIMENT OF THE "CHRISTOS"

Regardless of one's allegiance or otherwise to Jesus of Nazareth, it is generally agreed that his life was one of superhuman power, and that he performed healings of such a wondrous nature that they were regarded as miracles. These were so clearly the work of something greater than human wisdom that both he and his followers ascribed them to the eternal *christos*. He was so surrendered to the eternal *christos* that it was able to manifest more completely through him than through any other who ever lived before him or after.

Because the people considered him the embodiment of the *christos*, they changed his name to Jesus THE *CHRISTOS*, which was later shortened to "Jesu Christu," and still later Anglicized to "Jesus Christ."

The Bible maintains a deep silence on the formative years of Jesus between the ages of 12 and 30 years. It is thought by some that during this interim he took the overland route to the East and eventually found his way into India and Tibet. Whether he did or not, it is clearly evident from his teaching that in some way he had come under the influence of Buddhistic doctrine. Many of his sayings are pure Buddhism. Combining the stern asceticism of his native Judaism with the more liberal and deeply spiritual tenets of Buddhism, he had a broad-gauge approach to life that enabled him to castigate the hypocritical Pharisees for their pretenses, yet say to the adulterous woman, "Neither do I condemn thee." Moreover, he had acquired a knowledge of the *christos* which was far beyond that of his Judaistic teachers. He saw it as an ACTUAL FORCE working daily in the life of man, and as the key to freedom from the illnesses, poverty, and misery under which most of his compatriots lived.

One Sabbath when he went into the temple and was handed the Scriptures to read, as was the custom, he turned to a passage from the prophet Isaiah, and read that which we now give only in part, "For he hath anointed me to heal the sick, to open the eyes of the blind.

to preach deliverance to the captives." Then he closed the book, looked upon them, and said quietly, "This day is this scripture fulfilled in your ears." (Luke 4:18,21)

THE "CHRISTOS" WAS THE POWER IN JESUS

That day Jesus turned an abstraction to a reality. Wherever he had been during the eighteen years of his silence he, as an individual, had learned the secret of aligning himself with the Infinite Healing Presence; and he had come back to declare that the Eternal *christos* in man is able NOW, at THIS moment, in THIS place, to heal the sick and preach deliverance to the captives.

At another time, calling the *christos* "The Father," he said, "the Father in me, He doeth the works." (John 14:10) And shortly before he went to his death, he gave assurance to his disciples that this power was not his alone, but that they also had the power to do even greater works than he had done, through the indwelling *christos*.

It is a striking fact that whenever a person has come to see clearly the tremendous power of the Infinite Healing Presence, that person has been able to speak his word for the healing of conditions.

TO "HEAL" MEANS TO "MAKE WHOLE"

In this course we do not speak of "curing" but of "healing." The reason is that the word "heal" means "make whole." The person torn apart by his fears, hates, or greeds is not a whole person. He is a circle with one segment missing.

HEALING IS FROM WITHIN OUT

Healing is, first of all, something that happens at a man's center, in his thought-life. This reintegration, or making whole, then spreads out through his outer physical affairs into what the world recognizes as healing, but which is only the fruit of healing. The outer bodily or financial manifestation is only the shadow thrown on the outer screen of one's affairs by the healing or making whole of the inner man. The healing, then, is the healing of the false inward belief; the manifestation in form of this changed belief is the outer healing, fruit of the new belief.

Quite naturally, one is delighted at this manifestation, for we are all human enough to desire physical betterment; but here, in this first lesson, the student is warned that he MUST know where the REAL healing takes place; otherwise he will find himself treating conditions instead of causes. For example, in the Sermon on the Mount (Matt. 5-7) Jesus was trying to show the people the inner, hidden PRIN-CIPLE of wealth, but they had their minds set on money, which is only the outer token. This led him to give utterance to the basic principle, "Seek ye first the Kingdom of God and his righteousness [right thinking] and all these things shall [as the natural sequence] be added unto you." (Matt. 6:33)

The person who catches only a little of the SCIENCE OF MIND is likely to fall into the error of thinking that all he has to do is to THINK of health or prosperity and it will be his. We wish that were so, but unfortunately (or fortunately) it is not. Millions of persons think on these things; yet nothing happens to change their condition.

BEGIN NOW TO USE THIS PRINCIPLE

We close this lesson with the suggestion that you select some one thing, perhaps more, but at least one thing which you desire to see manifested before the conclusion of the course. You may hold it in mind or write it down to make it definite. After you have selected it, say quietly to yourself:

This experience exists NOW for me in the Infinite Mind. Each day I grow in the understanding of the supreme Law, which brings it forward into manifestation. I do not try to force it; I LET it come forth through my awakening consciousness, and give thanks for it even before I see it in form.

SPECIAL HELPS IN STUDYING THE LESSON

These study-helps have been carefully prepared to help you get the most out of this course.

QUESTIONS

Educators have found that a series of questions enables the student to get a complete picture of the material studied. You will find the questions accompanying each lesson highly valuable in uncovering concepts which you might otherwise pass by.

We advise that you first study the lesson carefully, then put it aside, write the answers to the questions, and, finally, *check your answers by the lesson.*

Keep the answers as a running commentary on the course *for your own benefit.* At its conclusion you will find that they have become a record of your own growth in consciousness.

(If you wish credit for the course, please request at the end of the twelve weeks a special set of questions.)

1. Name and explain the two phases of man's mind, giving the chief characteristics of each.
2. What is the interpretation of "Lord" as usually used in the Bible?
3. Explain the *christos.*
4. Why do we prefer to use the term "heal" rather than "cure"?
5. Where does the real healing take place?

WRITING SUGGESTION

Make a list of the conditions in your life that you wish to eliminate and of the new conditions that you wish to bring in.

Take an impersonal look at your thoughts and actions and make a list of those that you think should be dropped and those that should be cultivated.

Do you see any relationship between the two lists?

READING SUGGESTIONS

It is not imperative that the student read the books suggested for collateral reading, but we strongly recommend that he do so for deeper insight into the subjects treated.

The books suggested may be available in your public library. If not, they may be purchased from our Book Department. Please consult our *Book Catalogue.*
Frederick Bailes, *Your Mind Can Heal You,* Ch. I
Emmet Fox, *The Sermon on the Mount,* Ch. VI
Margery Wilson, *Your Personality and God,* Ch. VII

THOUGHT-TRAINING FOR THE WEEK

Watch for evidences, familiar and unfamiliar, of Wisdom at work in trees, stars, animals; and remind yourself that this same Wisdom is working in your body and your affairs.

A DAILY THOUGHT

Let this be your daily thought during the week that you study this lesson:
When things go wrong, some people look outside them-selves for the cause; the wise man looks within.

A DAILY SELF-TREATMENT
(To be spoken quietly and thoughtfully each morning and evening)

"I face the future with happy expectancy, with wonder. I wonder what new experiences of the good, the joyous, the enriching, lie in wait for me. I wonder what new persons will be drawn into my life, what new stores of health and vitality will be opened, what new depths of understanding will be uncovered within me.

"The future lies before me, 'stretched in smiling repose.' It is an unmarked, unmarred page. My thought is my pen, and life is what I write. No one else can write upon that page; therefore, I choose to know this day that the experiences that lie before me will be the best that I have ever known."

SCIENCE OF MIND

Home-Study Extension Course

(copyright 1951)

by

DR. FREDERICK BAILES

LESSON II

THOUGHT AND ITS POWER

A beginning student often says, "Wouldn't it be presumptuous of me to think that MY thought has such tremendous penetrating power that it could actually make alterations in the tissues of the body, and thus induce healing?"

It would. But his question shows that he does not yet understand the healing process. Perhaps the following illustration will show what we mean.

WHY OUR THOUGHT HAS POWER

The individual might be likened to an electric light bulb. The light manifests through it, but is NOT produced by it. Far back in the mountains are great lakes held back by giant dams. The lake water is diverted so as to run over turbine blades which are so tied in with generators that electricity is produced. This electricity, conducted through high tension wires, passes through transformers which step it down until it can pass through ordinary house wires. Then it is led into the tiniest wire of all, the wire within the light bulb. It cannot be contained within this tiny wire; and so, to describe the process somewhat roughly and unscientifically, it bursts forth into light inside the bulb.

The little bulb would, indeed, be presumptuous to say, "Look what I am doing!" Yet, it is well to remember that all the tremendous reserve of electricity would be useless for lighting without that tiny bulb. It is the interaction of the two which produces the result.

The Infinite Healing Presence is a surging Power. In a co-operative movement it finds outlet through an ordinary person. Each needs the other, and there must be tight connections between them. Just as there may be plenty of electricity flowing along the wires, but, because of imperfect connections, no light, so the degree of oneness between the healing *christos* and the individual determines the extent of the manifestation.

When Jesus said, "I and the Father are One," he evidently referred to this close connection, which explains the almost perfect flow of Divine Power through him. The degree to which the student can be brought to think in agreement with the Infinite thinking will determine the power which accompanies his spoken word.

MATERIALISTIC VS. SPIRITUAL THINKING

At this point we should begin to understand the meaning of spiritual thinking. This does not mean "goody-goody" or sanctimonious thinking. It has nothing to do with church attendance or Bible reading, although both of these exercises are desirable as aids in cultivating a higher consciousness; but a person may never enter a church yet be a deeply spiritual thinker.

Spiritual thinking is that method of thought which brushes aside the surface, apparent, physical interpretation of things, and sees into the spiritual reality beneath. Materialistic thinking is occupied with what it can see, taste, smell, hear, and handle. It accepts only that which can be mathematically demonstrated, or proved, in the laboratory. God has never been seen; His existence cannot be proved; therefore, the materialist will not accept the concept.

The spiritual thinker, however, has had experiences within the depth of his own inner self. These inner communings cannot be demonstrated in the laboratory; yet they have brought him certain states of peace, perhaps mastery over his lesser self; and so he is willing to believe that he has established some sort of contact with Something or Someone beyond it all.

The materialist believes in the surgeon's knife, but not in the two-edged sword of Truth. He can see the one, but for him the other may not exist. Many materialists have high, unselfish ideals, but materialism carried to its logical ultimate would draw man back to the level of the animal, for if life has no spiritual values which endure into our unseen life beyond the grave, man's smartest philosophy would be damned.

There is the person who says, "Look out for yourself. Do the other fellow before he does you. Money is your only friend. They won't ask you HOW you got it, but they'll look up to you if you have it. Ideals are all right to talk about, but this is a dog-eat-dog world, and you had better get the first bite."

The spiritual thinker places a higher value on ideals (unseen) than on material advantage (seen). He may be, and often is, a highly successful business man; but he places a much higher value on honor, integrity, his given word, truth, and fair dealing than on his success. We do not lose sight of the fact that there are many persons who belong in the two categories, but we have drawn the picture of the two types in order to make the distinction clear.

THOUGHTS BECOME THINGS

One of the fundamentals of this science is that man's inner world of thought is translated into his outer world of things. There is no inner yardstick to measure the quality, depth, or height of man's thinking; but as water cannot rise higher than its source, man's world of affairs can rise no higher than its inner source. Now, it follows that the higher the quality of the thought, the higher will be the manifestation. If so, what is the highest thought of which man is capable?

The answer must be that his loftiest thought is that which is concerned with the ideals we have just mentioned; and even higher are those thoughts which center themselves on the spiritual, on God, on the Intelligence which obviously lies within all nature, breathing through it. But what do we, or can we, know about such a Supreme Intelligence?

WHAT CAN WE KNOW OF GOD?

In the first place, no one has ever seen God. All we can do is to deduce something about the nature of the Infinite by watching closely the signs of His (or Its) handiwork. We all are impressed by the beauty of the sunset, of an orchid, or of the cool serenity of the moon on a cloudless night. But these might be only subjective impressions which may not disclose anything about the nature of the Infinite.

SCIENCE SEES INTELLIGENCE IN THE UNIVERSE

The persons who should be able to tell us more are the scientists who have spent a lifetime delving into the mysteries of nature. These men have roamed outer space through giant telescopes, peered into the heart of the atom through microscopes, and cut deep into living tissue to probe the mysteries of circulation; they have dissected the cell to learn the exact number of chromosomes in the different living species, and have gone into the brain to dissect the way nerve energy flows; and they have studied the composition, weight, and speed of those immense worlds which are only pinpoints of light in the sky.

GOD IS ORDER

These men, almost without exception, have spoken of the marvelous order and regularity revealed by their studies, and of the mathematical exactness with which everything seems to be put together. They have declared that ORDER seems to be one of the first laws of the universe.

GOD IS HARMONY

Coupled with this is a second thing that impresses us. It is that since HARMONY seems to be an undertone throughout the universe, this also can be said to be a characteristic of the Infinite.

GOD IS POWER

POWER needs no argument. It is evident that tremendous currents of POWER operate to keep the entire universe of suns, stars, and planets on their courses. The power in a tree root, referred to in the Introduction, is another example.

GOD IS WISDOM

WISDOM, the *christos*, has already been mentioned. The wisdom that guides a root to seek nutriment, which enables the flower or the tree to maintain life and grow, must be God-Wisdom, since it cannot lie in the root itself. The wisdom that enables the heart to beat regularly, the cells to select the proper nutritive elements from the blood, the wisdom that guides the processes of digestion, the marvelous chemistry of the endocrine glands which assembles simple materials such as food particles, and combines them into complex hormones—this is God-Wisdom.

GOD IS LOVE

And what shall be said of Love? God IS LOVE; yet we cannot imagine the Infinite to be softly sentimental in any maudlin manner. Love is a sincere WELL-WISHING for another, which provides the means for the greatest growth and expansion of the beloved. This the Infinite quite evidently has; for the love of God is evidenced in every law, every power, every attribute which man finds within himself or at his disposal, enabling him to "rise upon the stepping stones of his dead self to higher things."

Man makes a mistake when he thinks that the only love is that easy-going fondness which gives in to another person's pleading even when his better judgment tells him that his indulgence will not benefit the one concerned.

These, then, are some of the qualities and characteristics of the Infinite which are based upon reasonable assumptions. There are several others, as Life, Truth, Beauty, Self-sufficiency, Light, Holiness (wholeness), Justice, which can be deduced by the student through careful, logical thinking. Those we have stressed are sufficient for the purposes of this course.

MAN REPRODUCES THE DIVINE NATURE

It has been said that man is created in the image and likeness of

God. It would be absurd to think that there is any physical resemblance; therefore, it must be that man re-enacts the divine nature, and that in some way he is in the small what God is in the large. This which is true of God must also be true of man. By this we mean that man's true nature must be a reproduction of God's nature. This is the foundation of the belief in man's right to spiritual healing.

To return to the subject of man's highest thought: we have said that the higher the thought, the higher the manifestation. Thoughts which are God-like should produce results which are more than human; therefore, when man's thoughts are allowed to rest upon the Order, Harmony, Wisdom, Power, and Love which characterize the Infinite, and when he cultivates these qualities in himself, he will tend to reproduce the divine creativeness in his own affairs.

TREATMENT—A TURNING TOWARD PERFECTION

The wrong way to treat a physical illness would be to center the thought upon the pain and distress and the incurable side of the picture. This would be the way of the world. The SCIENCE OF MIND way is to turn immediately AWAY from all the physical symptoms, and focus the mind on our concept of God and of ourselves as reproducing His nature. We turn our thoughts toward that which is the very essence of order and harmony, for illness is DIS-order and IN-harmony. We turn away from the weakness evident in this body, and fill our thoughts with the Power which knows no limit, which twirls the planets on their axes and steers them in their courses around the sun.

We should put away all thought of the curability or incurability of this condition, and know that we are dealing with a Power which is limitless. We should stop thinking of the fact that the doctor has said, "I can do no more," and fill our thoughts with the contemplation of the Christ-Wisdom which has the exact knowledge of every step of the building process which creates brand-new cells, each stamped with Wisdom's own perfection.

TREATING FOR HEALTH

In treating ourself or others we turn away from things of earth, no matter how valid they seem to be, to "heaven": that is, to our highest possible concept. Illness is never healed by our continued contemplation of it in ourself or others; it is healed by quickly turning our thought to the great unblemished, unsick, unafraid Intelligence within, the Intelligence which formed the body in the first place, and which certainly knows how to rebuild and restore it. In later lessons we shall describe the exact technique of treatment so that the student may learn the definite procedure to follow; but at this stage it is necessary first to know the fundamentals which underlie all successful treatment, and we have just stated one of them.

TREATING FOR PROSPERITY

In like manner, one would never be able successfully to treat for prosperity if his thought were held steadily on the things he does NOT have. This suggests stringency. He must learn how to turn, instead, toward that which is forever self-sufficient, which knows its own sufficiency, and which calls upon its own inexhaustible resources whenever anything is needed in manifestation.

ELIMINATE NEGATIVE SPEECH

"Set a watch, O Lord, before my mouth; keep the door of my lips" (Psa. 141:3) is a verse that embodies another fundamental of successful treatment. We cannot always check our thought, because it is so lightning-fast that it is there before we notice it; but we can school ourselves NEVER TO GIVE UTTERANCE to that which is negative.

Too often we are led into the discussion of the troubles of others. We talk of a neighbor who has lost his job, or whose business has failed, or who has great difficulty making ends meet. In most communities these are the staples of conversation. We fail to see that we give reality to such conditions in others by taking part in such conversations. In doing this, we give these negative appearances reality in our own belief; and since nothing can happen to us except that in which we believe, we lay the foundation for the same experience in our own lives.

It is not always easy to refrain from such discussion in a group, or with some person who eagerly seizes upon every misfortune of his own or others as a topic of conversation; yet it is vitally necessary that we dissociate ourselves from such a consciousness. The student will have to devise his own method of discouraging such talk without hurting the feelings of his friends, or without being considered unsympathetic; but he will soon learn ways to turn the conversation in other directions. If he finds it impossible to shake a person loose from his morbid dwelling on the seamy side of life, he can say as little as possible to him, or else avoid meeting him.

WATCH YOUR WORDS

The chief thing for our liberation, however, is that we check ourselves whenever we catch ourselves starting such subjects. Students tell us that they never dreamed how much of their conversation was taken up with the morbid experiences of life until they started to "keep the door of their lips."

The world seems to have a hankering for the negative. This can be easily observed by sitting quietly in an ordinary group and listening to the discussion. Much of it centers around "my" operation, So-and-So's drinking, the accident at the corner, the divorce of John and Joan, the children's measles, the cancer drive, and the failure of the boss to appreciate John's excellent work.

The student of the SCIENCE OF MIND need not be a prig; neither is it necessary that he sit tight-lipped and disapproving at the discussion; but he will be cultivating his own spiritual consciousness if he endeavors cheerfully to turn the conversation in a positive, optimistic direction. There are so many happy, hopeful things going on that he will have no difficulty in doing this if he "sets a watch before his mouth."

HANDLE NEGATIVE EXPERIENCE IN A POSITIVE WAY

"But," someone says, "what if my husband HAS just lost his job, or we simply can NOT afford that television set? Are we to ignore these apparent facts?"

Not at all! But there is a positive and a negative way of discussing them. Losing a job may be regarded either as an ending or a beginning. The difference between an optimist and a pessimist is seen in the way they discuss any subject. Suppose each has a glass of water, half gone. The pessimist says, "Too bad, my glass is already half empty!" The optimist says, "Good, my glass is still half full!" Same amount of water but two ways of regarding it.

The pessimist says, "I've lost my job; whatever will I do now?" The optimist says, "Well, that's the end of that. I wonder what bigger opportunity lies before me?"

In the SCIENCE OF MIND we never say, "I can't afford that item." Neither do we deceive ourselves or others about our inability to buy it; we take the constructive, hopeful view by saying, "I think we'll be able to get that television set before long."

The student has made considerable progress when he comes to see that no one can ever separate us from our good BUT WE OUR-SELVES. Man never is displaced from any desirable situation until he has let his MENTAL fingers loosen their hold upon it. He or she may have become MENTALLY separated from the loved one through carelessness or inattention or "taking him for granted," through complaining of monotony in the job or about his fellow workers, or about the job in general. He may MENTALLY separate himself from his position through fear and anxiety, or through the belief that he is not doing good enough work or that he is doing too much work for the pay he receives, or through any one of a hundred other mental states. Subconsciously he MENTALLY lets go of his job when he has outgrown it.

RIGHT PLACEMENT

The positive way of regarding this situation is by saying, "I am always in my right place. I am always at the place where I belong by right of my consciousness. If I have become separated from the job through my negative approach, I start right now to learn. I begin now to alter my inner consciousness so that I AM steadily united with my good. If I have outgrown this opportunity, I know that another and better job is now awaiting me, one for which I am better qualified. I resolutely put behind me any complaint or resentment, for this is a new beginning, in which life moves onto a higher level."

Then, with a watch set upon his lips, he studiously avoids expressing rancor, bitterness, or discouragement. To friends who would commiserate with him, he turns a deaf ear, refusing to listen to their, "It's a dirty shame, John!"

Why does he do this? Wouldn't it be more honest to say, "Yes, I got a raw deal," because in reality that was what happened? The answer is, "No," because it would only tend to perpetuate the state of mind that led to his dismissal. If he sees WHY and HOW we attract experiences, he will honestly know that we unconsciously ATTRACT our own "raw deals."

There are two ways of reacting to misfortune. The negative is, "WHY should this happen to me?" The positive is, "WHAT has this to teach me?" or "WHAT good can it yield to me?"

EVERY EFFECT HAS AN ADEQUATE CAUSE

The student who has absorbed the teaching so far knows that whether he can trace it or not, it MUST have been some loosening of his MENTAL fingers that led to his separation from his good. Nothing in his life ever comes by chance; everything comes by the Law of Cause and Effect. Nothing ever just "happens" to us. For every effect there is always an adequate and consistent cause.

We deny this law when we complain about what life hands us, and thus we place ourselves in the position where our next step may lead to our becoming a discouraged whiner and complainer. If this is allowed to go on, we can develop a fully matured persecution complex, which can mean the end of all constructive thinking and consequently of all advancement.

LOOK WITHIN FOR CAUSES

The untutored or unscientific thinker always looks outside himself for the cause of his miseries. The person who is spiritually scientific always looks within for the basic reason. Even when he seems unable to locate the origin of his trouble, he sticks to the fact that his outer world of affairs is only his inner world of consciousness brought down into form. This checks his complaint at the outset. It makes of every unhappy condition not an ending but a beginning. It keeps him with a constructive view of life, and continually turns him away from the morbid. It keeps him from hating anyone, because even though some other person's actions seem unfair, he knows that something within himself drew forth these actions, and he determines to weed the garden of his thought so that it will not occur again.

The place where his progress starts is at his lips where he checks the expression of his negative thoughts. As he practices this, he will soon notice that this sort of thought comes less and less frequently. Ultimately his new tendency of mind will become the starting point of his progress.

But until this happens, he can make a good start at the point where his thoughts form into words, at his lips; and he must PRACTICE it. One knows that he could not become a facile violin player without daily practice. Should we expect proficiency in living unless we practice? Since assiduous practice of the techniques WILL make an accomplished violinist, so will daily practice of spiritual techniques lead to happy, healthy, successful living.

SPECIAL HELPS IN STUDYING THE LESSON

These study-helps have been carefully prepared to help you get the most out of this course.

QUESTIONS

Educators have found that a series of questions enables the student to get a complete picture of the material studied. You will find the questions accompanying each lesson highly valuable in uncovering concepts which you might otherwise pass by.

We advise that you first study the lesson carefully, then put it aside, write the answers to the questions, and, finally, *check your answers by the lesson.*

Keep the answers as a running commentary on the course *for your own benefit.* At its conclusion you will find that they have become a record of your own growth in consciousness.

1. Why does man's thought have power?
2. What is the underlying difference between spiritual and material thinking?
3. What does our outer world of affairs (state of health, finances, personal relationships, etc.) reveal about the state of our thought life?
4. What does it mean to say that man is created in the image and likeness of God?
5. What must always precede the outer experience?

WRITING SUGGESTION

Set down the five attributes of God as given in this lesson, add others from your own observation, experience, or other source of knowledge, and list under each as many evidences of it as you can. You will find it helpful to keep this in a convenient place and add to it throughout the course.

READING SUGGESTIONS

It is not imperative that the student read the books suggested for collateral reading, but we strongly recommend that he do so for deeper insight into the subjects treated.

The books suggested may be available in your public library. If not, they may be purchased from our Book Department. Please consult our *Book Catalogue*.

> Frederick Bailes, *Your Emotions Can Kill or Cure,* and
> *Your Mind Can Heal You,* Ch. II
> Claude Bristol, *The Magic of Believing*
> Emmet Fox, *The Sermon on the Mount,* Ch. III
> Margery Wilson, *Your Personality and God,* Ch. IV

THOUGHT-TRAINING FOR THE WEEK

As a starting point to eliminating negative thought, eliminate negative speech. "Set a watch before my mouth; keep the door of my lips." A simple test for positive speech is this: Do I want this thing that I am saying about myself (or about another) realized in *my* life?

A DAILY THOUGHT

Let this thought be your daily thought during the week that you study this lesson:

> Our outer world of affairs is our inner world of consciousness in form.

A DAILY SELF-TREATMENT
(To be spoken quietly and thoughtfully each morning and evening)

"My mind is an inlet of the Infinite Ocean of Mind. In its depths lies all the knowledge of past, present, and future. In it are deep levels untouchable by any surface influences. In it lies the healing power of the Infinite Christ, that 'Light which lighteth every man who cometh into the world.' In it lies the answer to every problem, freedom from every fetter, healing for every condition, balm for every hurt.

"My mind, as an inlet of the Infinite Ocean of Mind, has power to renew itself, to alter its patterns, to rise into the place of dominance over illness, lack, or inharmony. My mind is God's Mind in me this day."

SCIENCE OF MIND

Home-Study Extension Course

(copyright 1951)

by

DR. FREDERICK BAILES

LESSON III

THE FOCUS OF ATTENTION

As previously indicated, the early lessons of this course deal with the basic, underlying mental attitudes out of which will come the specific methods of treating definitely for specific results. Extending the thought of our last lesson we come to another fundamental statement: NEVER SAY A THING ABOUT YOURSELF WHICH YOU DO NOT WANT TO SEE REALIZED IN YOUR LIFE.

NEVER BELITTLE YOURSELF

In speaking of setting a watch upon our lips, we refer now to a very common practice, that of belittling ourself, our talents and abilities, our achievements. It is a minimizing of our strong points and a ballooning of our weak points. A little of this may be due to modesty; but the larger proportion actually grows out of a general sense of inferiority, and is done for the purpose of having someone else bolster our morale. The person who does this is not sure of himself. He craves reassurance and seeks this way of finding it or having it handed to him.

It is not easy to plunge to the center of the problem and immediately build an awareness of our own worth, but we can approach it by practicing a procedure which would be quite natural for us if we already had the inner consciousness of our true worth.

- 1 -

ACT OUT THE PART OF THE PERSON
YOU WANT TO BE

We can decide what sort of person we would like to be and begin at once to act the part. One who does this usually finds that he comes to think within himself as he wants to think. We are, however, under no circumstances, to act the part WITH THE INTENTION OF IMPRESSING OTHERS. What others think of us at this stage is not important; and while we might succeed in fooling them, we could never fool ourselves. It's ourselves, only, that we are dealing with now, and we must deal honestly. What we think of ourselves is the chief thing.

If, as sometimes happens, we should have a return of that feeling that we're "not so much," we must instantly make up our minds that we will never again voice it. This will stop the drift toward the negative.

We must never forget that the power of the spoken word is far greater than we imagine. Even though he does not fully believe the truth of what he says, the person who insists, "I have no personality," or "I am not attractive," is giving himself a treatment from the negative side, which will tend to make him unattractive.

To say, "I am never able to hold a job," will set a current of energy in motion which will continue to result in his losing jobs. "I always get the bad breaks," or "I was a fool to quit that job," or "I always do the wrong thing at the right time," are all expressions which gain terrific force once they are put into words, especially if they are repeated from time to time.

WE ARE TODAY WHAT WE
THOUGHT YESTERDAY

There is a reason for this. Today is the finished product of yesterday's or last year's thought. Today's thought, even now passing through the loom of mind, will become the pattern of tomorrow's or next year's experience. That which we now are thinking will take form, sometime, somewhere.

If we hope to get free from those negative, unwanted conditions we have been voicing, we must make our start TODAY by changing our thought. And if we have not yet advanced to the point where we have thorough control over our thoughts, we can, at least to a large degree, control our speech; therefore, TODAY, we refuse to give utterance to that which we now know will only perpetuate our unwanted past experiences.

TURN AWAY FROM PAST FAILURES

The person who reaches backward to stress the points at which he made mistakes or a wrong choice, or failed to impress others, thereby places those negative things in the forefront of his consciousness, and his loom of mind has no choice but to weave them into similar experiences tomorrow. It is done unto us as we believe; and if we believe that we made blunders yesterday, then it follows that we shall make blunders tomorrow, for we are expressing our belief in blunders. If we believe people were not attracted to us yesterday, then we believe they will not be attracted tomorrow. And so it is with every negative belief.

This is why the student, from now on, should speak only of those things he wants to see realized in his life.

TURN TO PAST SUCCESSES
NO MATTER HOW SMALL

Having assumed a positive attitude, we can now recall the times when we made the right decisions or when someone showed a decided liking for our company, or when we made the right choice or got the "good breaks." We may think of the times when we showed to good advantage when competing with others; we may recall sincere compliments paid us. And, being very careful not to become a boasting bore, we may even speak of our achievements; for we are now trying hard to reverse our previous negative underlying trend of thought, and anything that feeds our belief in our true worth is grist for our mill.

We call to mind ANY compliment ever given us, even those we felt were insincere; for, although the insincere person thought he was "putting one over" on us, we turn it inside out and read our own meaning into it, knowing that any action, any utterance, becomes to us that which we want to make it.

Now the student may make a quiet decision: "I will never say a thing about myself that I do not want to see realized in my life." This one principle has changed the lives of thousands.

LIFE PAYS US WHAT WE ASK

Life is never unfair to us. We are unfair to ourselves. Ours is the choice—we may offer ourselves in the bargain basement or in the exclusive section, and Life is not only willing to pay, IT HAS NO ALTERNATIVE BUT TO PAY the exact price we set upon ourselves. It can pay no more, no less, because it is as impartial as the mirror, which must reflect exactly that which is placed before it. It is as impersonal as the loom, which must weave into cloth the threads that are given it, be they cheap white cotton or costly threads of silk.

When we come to see this, life no longer will seem harsh and cruel to us. Our world will change as our ideas concerning ourselves change. So never be afraid to think highly of your value.

This implies making ourselves valuable. The shirker, constantly watching the clock or giving inadequate service, should not expect to lie on his back, filling his thought with the picture of his worth, and imagining that Infinite Mind will formulate this latter picture into form.

One may fool his employer—he can never fool this Law. He is avoiding his rightful responsibilities; therefore, Mind will give him what he most deeply wants—a life devoid of responsibility. Since life's biggest rewards are coupled with biggest responsibilities, in avoiding responsibility he is avoiding reward.

POWER FLOWS TO THE FOCUS OF ATTENTION

It might be well at this point to consider the difficulty of constantly maintaining positive attitudes. As human beings, subject to the limitations of our common humanity, we find that, in spite of our earnest desire to maintain the highest level of thinking, negative thoughts continue to creep up on us. When the untutored find the old pattern showing up from time to time, they are likely to abandon their efforts in disgust. In the SCIENCE OF MIND, however, we know that this is neither disastrous nor final, for POWER FLOWS TO THE FOCUS OF ATTENTION.

To help the student understand what we mean by "the focus of attention," we shall begin with a concrete example taken from our outer world. The student himself may illustrate this by standing at his front door and looking steadily at—let us say—an outstanding house-number directly across the street. He will see that number distinctly, because he is focusing his attention on it; but as he looks at it, without moving his eyes, he will also be conscious of things on either side. Those nearer the center of his vision, the house-numbers, will be somewhat clear, but objects in his marginal line of vision will shade and become increasingly vague as they are more to the right and to the left of the house-number, which is the focal point of his attention.

We shall now move to the world of thought. The chart below represents man's consciousness from one point of view. Man has central consciousness, and he has marginal consciousness. In his central consciousness are those things of which he is most vividly aware and which obtrude themselves upon his thought most often or most forcefully. His marginal consciousness bears upon those things of which he is only dimly aware.

FOCUS OF ATTENTION CHART

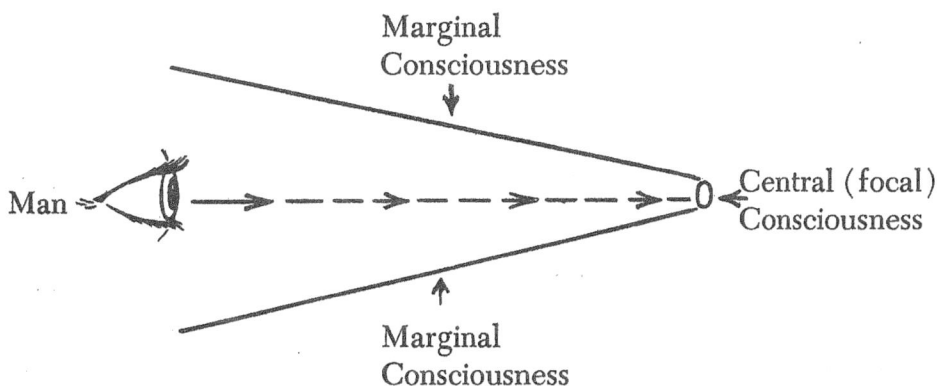

THE LAW OF ATTRACTION

MAN TENDS TO ATTRACT THAT WHICH HE LOVES, FEARS, OR STEADILY EXPECTS: that is, those things which he keeps at his central (focal) consciousness.

In the past he has feared certain negative experiences and, quite logically, he has attracted them. But the student has made up his mind that from now on, he is definitely going to love his most cherished desire above everything else; therefore, as often as possible, he is going to draw it into the focus of his attention. There will come times when the negative will edge toward the center, but the instant he notices this, he will again bring back into focus that good which he wishes, and surround it with his love. Gradually he will notice that the good, more and more, tends to stay at the center, while the negative tends to fade away.

MAN'S MIND IS OF THE ONE MIND

There is a good reason why "Power flows to the focus of attention." The mind of man is not something separate; it is part of the One Intelligence, which formed and sustains the universe. Man's brain structure is the best on earth, far surpassing that of the highest animal; yet it has certain limitations. While man's mind is historical, in that it can look back and recall the past, it is not prophetic: that is, it cannot look forward and with any certainty foretell the future. Though it has other limitations, we mention this one just as an illustration.

Limited as man's mind is, however, it is still a part of the Infinite Intelligence, and is forever united with it. This Infinite Intelligence, carrying all ideas in their perfection, is like an ageless river ever flowing through the brain of man.

THERE IS A "KNOWER" WITHIN US

All man's future inventions and discoveries are at this moment in that river. As it flows through the brains of men whose habitual thought tends toward some particular idea and concept, those men catch and register new ideas in line with their concepts. That is why men on opposite sides of the earth who have never known each other often come forth simultaneously with the same invention, the same discovery, the same story theme. Each one believes that he, personally, originated the idea; but no human ever really originates. He merely—to change the analogy—tunes in on ideas carried in the One Great Originating Mind.

INFINITE CREATIVENESS INVESTS
MAN'S THOUGHT

Earlier we said that man is in the small what God is in the large.

Creativeness is of God. Man's thought is creative, because God's thought flows through it, as electrical current flows through a microphone, magnifying the voice far beyond its normal power. The thoughts of a person are small and weak in comparison with those of the Infinite; but being of the same nature as that of the Infinite, they are "boosted" to something far beyond the human. Thus, when the Great Teacher said, "The Father (*christos*) in me, He it is that doeth the works," he was pointing the way for ANYONE to have power.

If we imagine our chart illustrating the focus of attention as a funnel through which all the power and creativeness of the Infinite flows, then we can see that when a man draws a particular idea to the center of his thought, it is flowed through by that central stream of the Infinite power. Those thoughts that are along the margins of consciousness are not subjected to this creative flow to the same degree. It follows, therefore, that the fleeting, dimly conceived thought has less power than that which is steadily held toward the center.

We can make this even more emphatic: THAT WHICH LIES AT THE FOCUS OF MAN'S ATTENTION IS BOUND TO COME FORTH. ANY IDEA HELD WITH QUIET, UNFORCED STEADINESS WILL ASSUREDLY MANIFEST.

THE DOMINANT PATTERN EMERGES

This does not mean that one idea must be held to the exclusion of all others, nor does it mean that our desired manifestation will not come forth if our thinking is a mixture of positive and negative. Since man is far from perfect, the thinking of the best and most successful persons is mixed; but it has been proved that, despite varied thinking, if one's dominant desire is held more or less steadily at the center of his attention and affection, it will manifest. "Let us not be weary in well-doing, for in due season we shall reap, if we faint not." (Gal. 6:9)

DIRECTING THE FOCUS OF ATTENTION

Another basic attitude which makes for success in demonstration is that of love. This word has been thrown about so lightly, even loosely, and has been surrounded by such an atmosphere of "stickiness" that we hesitate to use it. It might be better to say that all hostility must be removed from the heart if one would make demonstrations. Since we have seen that harmony is basic in the universe, it follows that hostility throws us out of tune with the creative flow. "Love is the fulfilling of the Law." Hostility is the obstructing of the Law.

It is apparent that hatred and love cannot occupy the same place at the same moment. It should, therefore, be apparent that man cannot demonstrate his good while wishing that someone else be kept from HIS good. Grudges, resentment, and criticism can effectually stop our demonstration, because, as a rule, they are so intense that they automatically rush to the focus of attention.

To understand all would be to forgive all. If we could know all the influences that have played upon the person who has wronged us, we might understand why he has acted as he has. If those same influences had assailed us with equal force, we might have done just as he did. At any rate, harboring a grudge or a resentment will block our achievement of good. It is too high a price to pay. The person against whom hostility is held is not hurt by it; it is the person who harbors it who is the loser. The practice of the spirit of understanding will make us gentle. It is one of the most enriching attitudes one can cultivate.

THE SCIENCE OF MIND IS A WAY OF LIFE

It can be seen that the SCIENCE OF MIND involves one's whole way of life. It is impossible to cultivate love for mankind in general and at the same time retain a tiny corner of our thought for feelings of hostility toward an individual; for if, with all our good hanging in the balance, our hostility is still important enough or appealing enough for us to hang onto, it will also have an appeal powerful enough to color all the rest of our thinking, and effectually block our treatment for others and our pathway into the land of our heart's desire.

All that a person IS goes into his treatment. Not alone the words of his mouth must be acceptable, but also the meditation of his heart. (Psa. 19:14)

Some students want to be rid of their illnesses, their poverty, or some other handicap; yet at the same time they cling to their meannesses or their pet neuroses. This cannot be done. "Except man be born again, he cannot see the kingdom of God." (John 3:3) He not only cannot enter it; he cannot even see it. "Old things are passed away; all things are become new." (2 Cor. 5:17) He is born into a new way of life, a new way of thinking. Where this is done thoroughly, his eyes look out upon a different world. He is born again. He has become a new man in the *christos*.

There must be, for the student, a rightabout-face, an altering of his whole life; for he is now shifting his thought from the world's way to God's way; from the human, material way to the spiritual way. There must be sincerity of purpose when he takes the pathway to the fulfillment of his deepest desires, a clearing out of the old and a bringing in of the new. "Men do not put new wine into old bottles . . . but they put new wine into new bottles." (Matt. 9:17)

The SCIENCE OF MIND is not simply something added to our belief in order to make us well and prosperous. It demands all of the student. If he gives it, it will flood his life with the Good.

HABITS — A MATTER OF CONSCIOUSNESS

Students sometimes want to know whether they must give up certain habits in order to make their demonstration. We are not keepers of morals and, at this point, place no restrictions upon the student. We feel that each person can and will make his own decisions about his habits. The student probably will continue with whatever he is doing until he has a persistent uneasy feeling about it. Then, whatever he quits, or whatever new habit he takes on will be as a result of HIS OWN growing consciousness, and will therefore be right for him.

Standards of morals and ethics vary so much that no teacher can tell anyone what is "good" or "bad." To some, the eating of flesh is bad; to others the use of tea, coffee, tobacco, or alcohol is reprehensible. Habits which are accepted in some countries are frowned upon in others. It is not so long ago that a person would be refused membership in some churches unless he promised to forsake theater, cards, dancing. Today there is dancing at church socials. "There is nothing either good or bad [in itself] but thinking makes it so." Quite obviously this does not refer to gross sins but only to those debatable and minor details of one's personal life.

Each one must decide for himself. The only guide should be, "Does this practice hinder my spiritual unfoldment, or is it definitely destructive to me or to someone else?" If so, we would say that it would be better out of the life.

SPECIAL HELPS IN STUDYING THE LESSON

These study-helps have been carefully prepared to help you get the most out of this course.

QUESTIONS

Educators have found that a series of questions enables the student to get a complete picture of the material studied. You will find the questions accompanying each lesson highly valuable in uncovering concepts which you might otherwise pass by.

We advise that you first study the lesson carefully, then put it aside, write the answers to the questions, and, finally, *check your answers by the lesson*.

Keep the answers as a running commentary on the course *for your own benefit*. At its conclusion you will find that they have become a record of your own growth in consciousness.

1. What is a beginning step that we may take in building a consciousness of our true worth?
2. Explain "Power flows to the focus of attention."
3. Why is that which lies at the focus of man's attention *bound to come forth?*
4. Why is an attitude of love an absolute essential in the making of demonstrations?
5. Comment on "The Science of Mind involves the whole life."

WRITING SUGGESTION

Make a list of those desired conditions which you are going to keep in the main focus of your attention.

READING SUGGESTIONS

It is not imperative that the student read the books suggested for collateral reading, but we strongly recommend that he do so for deeper insight into the subjects treated.

The books suggested may be available in your public library. If not, they may be purchased from our Book Department. Please consult our *Book Catalogue.*

Frederick Bailes, "Stop Drifting and Start Driving"
Kahlil Gibran, *The Prophet,* "Self-Knowledge"
David Seabury, *How Jesus Heals Our Minds Today,*
297-317 and others
Margery Wilson, *Your Personality and God,* Ch. V

THOUGHT-TRAINING FOR THE WEEK

Do not say a thing about yourself that you do not want realized in your life.

A DAILY THOUGHT

Let this thought be your daily thought during the week that you study this lesson:

We attract what we love, fear, hate, or steadily expect.

A DAILY SELF-TREATMENT
(To be spoken quietly and thoughtfully each morning and evening)

"This day I increase my awareness of the River of Mind flowing in me. I am healed of the distortion which saw only the debris on the surface. My clearer vision now sees through to the Reality beneath, to the pure untainted streaming of the Infinite, and my healing is completed as I come alive to the River, as it is alive to me.

"The River of God's Perfect Mind manifests this day in me as life. It now overflows my consciousness as joy. It now bathes my entire being as peace. It now fills my every need and turns into a Niagara· of abundance. It is a river of physical healing to me and mine. My good is so great that it spills over into the lives of others and sets their good in motion. Thus I become a blessing to all who come in contact with me this day."

SCIENCE OF MIND

Home-Study Extension Course

(copyright 1951)

by

DR. FREDERICK BAILES

LESSON IV

THE TRINITY OF GOD
AND ITS COUNTERPART IN MAN

In this lesson the student is brought into a deeper and more metaphysical aspect of the SCIENCE OF MIND. It is urged that he study this lesson carefully, going over it several times, and then that he rewrite it for his own benefit. He must make very sure that he has a clear understanding of the difference between SPIRIT and MIND. Success in demonstration depends on this.

When the student has grasped the inner meaning of these terms, he will have a sense of authority when he speaks his word. He will no longer wonder whether results will follow; he KNOWS that they will, because he will have within himself the deep conviction of the power and reality of the thing he is working with. Once he has mastered this phase of it, the remainder of the course will fall naturally into place.

It is natural that man should want to draw into his experience those desirable things which are not there now. Thus every demonstration is an act of creation. That which man desires HAS TO BE CREATED. When we find the general principle of creation, we can apply it to create the particular. There is such a principle, of course, traceable throughout the universe. It is the selfsame principle and method through which our world came into being.

THE CREATIVE PROCESS

In *The Creative Process in the Individual,* Thomas Troward has done a masterly work of delineating this principle. We recommend that you add this book to your library, and study it carefully. Some may find it not an easy book to read; but return to it again and again, for it will amply repay the time and effort given to it.

Troward's book was written early in this century, before many of our scientific discoveries were made. Though some of the scientific terms he uses are now outmoded, his principle stands today stronger than when he advanced it; and modern scientists agree that the creative process he outlines might very well have been the one by which the universe was created. It is, therefore, a metaphysical principle in line with modern science. The student who masters Troward has a solid rock of metaphysical philosophy under his feet.

THERE IS ONLY ONE CREATIVE PROCESS

Troward's thesis is that there is ONLY ONE CREATIVE PROCESS IN THE UNIVERSE. It brought the world at large into being; every moment it is bringing man's personal world into being. By this process a star is created, or a body healed. In order to grasp this, the student will start with an inquiry into the nature of God, or, as Troward calls it, the Originating Intelligence.

Troward starts with the well-known fact that matter—even though it is hard and solid and has weight—is only energy or force in form. In the beginning it is quite evident that there was no universe in solid form; yet, all the material out of which the universe would be formed was present in an unformed state, as the unformed "Body of God." In the beginning there was only God—and NOTHING. The energy which caused the universe to be formed could only have been an energy which does not originate in the material sphere. Now, the only known form of energy which does not arise out of matter is—THOUGHT. But there were no people in existence; so the thought must have been that of an Infinite Thinker. The eminent physicist, Sir James Jeans, in a purely scientific way, arrives at this same conclusion as we shall show in our next lesson.

PRACTICAL RESULTS OF UNDERSTANDING THE TRINITY

The three-sided nature of Infinite Intelligence is somewhat difficult to comprehend. Perhaps a simple illustration will make it clear.

Think of a block of ice. We know it is ice and nothing else; yet it is water, and with a slight change can be steam.

Placed in a pail on a hot stove, the ice soon becomes water, which is ice at a higher molecular vibration; its molecules are moving at a higher rate than when it was ice.

More heat is applied, and the water now becomes steam, a still higher vibration. Thus there have been three different substances, each with a different name; yet they are all basically one, differing only in their vibratory rate.

Each functions differently from the other. As steam, this substance will clean the grease off an automobile motor, which ice or water will not do. Ice will keep fruit fresh, which steam will not do. Water will serve as the abode of fish, which neither steam nor ice will do.

SAME THING—DIFFERENT NAMES

Thus we have a diversity of name, form, and function for the same thing; yet under whatever name and whatever function it acts, its basic essential character is the same, namely H_2O.

Suppose we reverse the procedure. Invisible steam emerging from the kettle spout becomes visible vapor; passed over or through a cool coil, it becomes water; refrigerated, it becomes ice. Each gradation becomes more dense or "solid" than the preceding one.

Suppose we think of Spirit as the highest vibration in the Trinity, invisible like the steam in its activity. It selects what is to be done and initiates the Creative Cycle. Its decisions are not seen by us until

Mind, a lower vibration, manifests them by acting upon the Primary Unformed Substance to condense it into form, a still lower vibration. At this point the Creative Sequence has been completed.

We regret having to use such a crude analogy, but the Unseen must sometimes be depicted in terms of the seen, the Unknown in terms of the known, since man is still in that kindergarten stage of development where he must use the physical senses to interpret spiritual truth.

HOW THE CREATIVE CYCLE OPERATES

To apply this illustration, let us see how creation occurs, remembering that as God the Greater Trinity creates a universe, man the smaller trinity creates any good which he desires.

Spirit, Mind, and Unformed Substance, which we call Body, have always been. Physicists tell us that matter must always have been present in an unformed state. No one of the Three has created the others. There is equality among them since they have all been present throughout the eternity that is past, but there is a division of function for some inscrutable reason. (Troward speaks of Spirit *containing* the Primary Substance, and then *projecting*, or *evolving*, not creating it.)

Spirit exercises SELECTION by deciding that there shall be a formed universe. We may call Spirit the Architect. As part of its indivisible Being, the Architect has Mind the Builder, and Body, or Unformed Substance, the Building Materials.

In addition to its power of selection, Spirit possesses the power of INITIATIVE. It initiates the Creative Sequence by its "LET THERE BE." It then releases its Word completely to Mind the Builder, which obediently and without question accepts the decree and proceeds to carry it out. Mind molds the plastic, unresisting Primary Unformed Substance into the form of the idea expressed by Spirit, following with exactitude as though from a blueprint.

THOUGHTS ARE THINGS— THINGS ARE THOUGHTS

At this point we might observe that the thought of Spirit does not "influence" body to become a certain thing. Instead, the thought of Spirit actually BECOMES the form. Mind, the Fabricator, takes the original, identical idea or concept of Spirit and condenses it down into actual form; thus the form is the original idea lowered into visibility to us. It was just as real when it was only a concept; we humans, living in a world of sense, make the mistake of thinking it is real only when our sense organs can apprehend it.

Physicists say that all matter is nothing but FORCE condensed into form, and that electricity is the point at which force is turning into form. They say that electricity (in the electron) is force at its densest point, and is matter at its least dense point. The thoughts of Spirit and Mind are force; therefore, it is quite conceivable that the entire universe is the thought of God in visible form.

GOD IS ALL—AND IN ALL

Since both force and matter have been present from the remotest beginning, coequal phases of the Originating Intelligence, it is quite logical to assume that the entire universe, including us, can rightly be called the Body of God. From this point of view there was originally nothing but God; there is now nothing but God in changed form. God IS all, and IN all—in Him we live, move, and have our being. (Acts 17:28)

This is of the greatest importance, for he who understands this most clearly will do the best work in treating himself or others.

On the following page is a very important chart showing the Trinity and the Creative Process in both God and man. Those students who grasp its meaning and implications invariably produce effects far in advance of those who fail to do so; the more it is studied the more clearly is seen the relationship between the obedient response of this vast creative power to man's conscious choices. It removes treatment from a vague, hit-or-miss dependence upon "feeling" to an authoritative "knowing," such as the Infinite has when It says, "Let there be." We would suggest that this chart and lesson be studied EACH WEEK in addition to the lesson of that week.

THE TRINITY

The three phases of the Godhead, acting concurrently, consummate the one Creative Process. By this process God brought the universe into being. By this same process man brings his world into being.

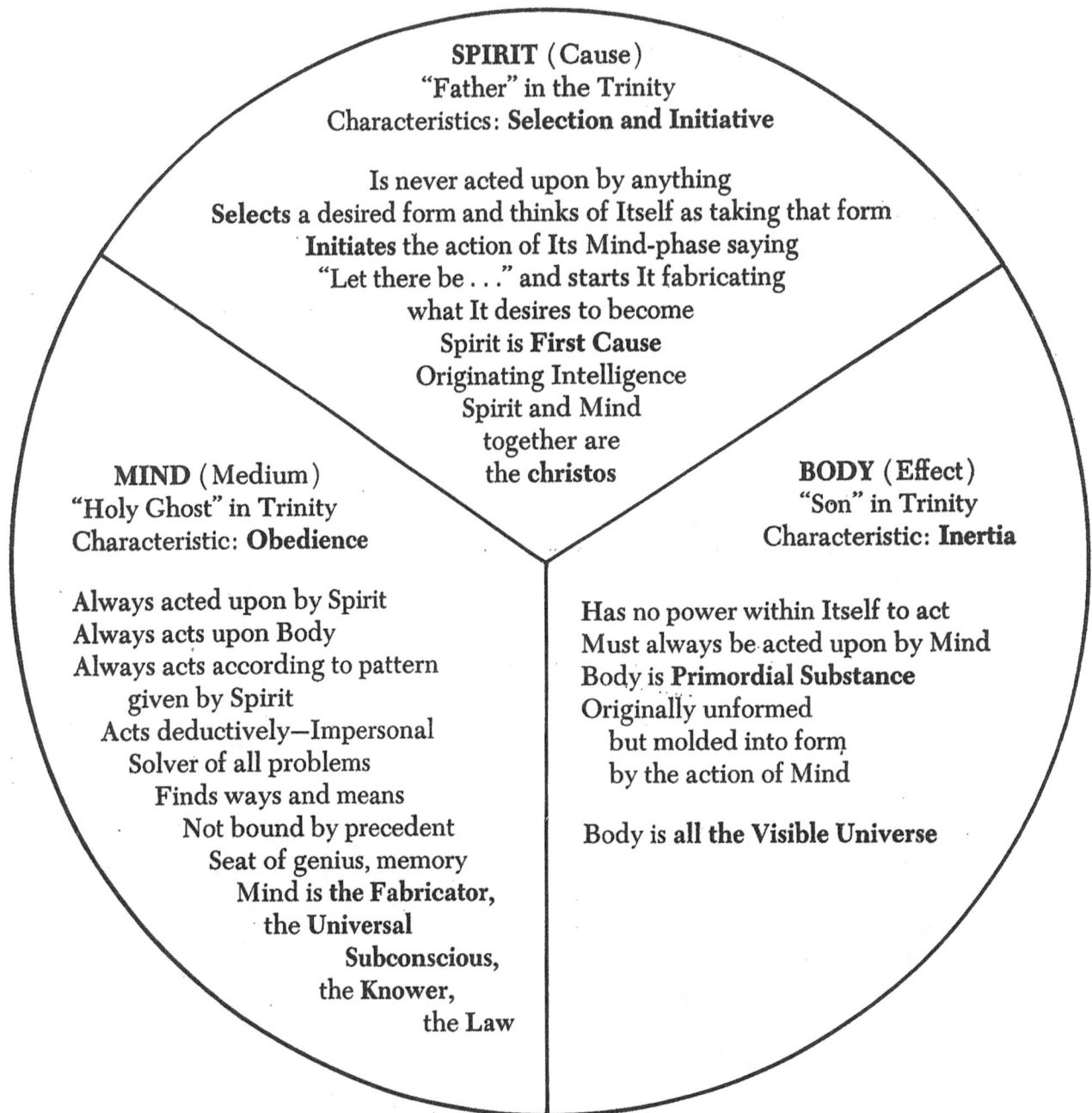

SPIRIT (Cause)
"Father" in the Trinity
Characteristics: **Selection and Initiative**

Is never acted upon by anything
Selects a desired form and thinks of Itself as taking that form
Initiates the action of Its Mind-phase saying
"Let there be . . ." and starts It fabricating
what It desires to become
Spirit is **First Cause**
Originating Intelligence
Spirit and Mind
together are
the **christos**

MIND (Medium)
"Holy Ghost" in Trinity
Characteristic: **Obedience**

Always acted upon by Spirit
Always acts upon Body
Always acts according to pattern
given by Spirit
Acts deductively—Impersonal
Solver of all problems
Finds ways and means
Not bound by precedent
Seat of genius, memory
Mind is **the Fabricator,**
the **Universal
Subconscious,**
the **Knower,**
the **Law**

BODY (Effect)
"Son" in Trinity
Characteristic: **Inertia**

Has no power within Itself to act
Must always be acted upon by Mind
Body is **Primordial Substance**
Originally unformed
but molded into form
by the action of Mind

Body is **all the Visible Universe**

Man selects a goal in his SURFACE mind and releases it to his DEEPER mind, which acts upon body to bring it into form. This is the Creative Cycle.

MAN IS ALSO A TRINITY OF SPIRIT, MIND, AND BODY

We have said before that man is in the small that which God is in the large. Man, therefore, is spirit, mind, and body, these three phases being characterized by the same qualities as those attributed to their Counterparts. The Body of the Originating Intelligence is the entire material universe. The body of man is more than his physical body; it is his entire environmental world as well. The subconscious mind of man, called in this course his DEEPER mind, corresponds to Mind in the Trinity. Man's conscious mind, called here his SUR-FACE mind, corresponds to Spirit in the Trinity.

This correspondence between man's body, mind, and spirit and those Counterparts in the Infinite God-Intelligence refers to their mode of action. Man's body is characterized by inertia, as is Body in the Divine Trinity. Man's DEEPER mind acts ALWAYS in complete obedience to the decrees of his SURFACE mind, or Spirit. Man's spirit, or SURFACE mind, has the power to select, initiate, and decree what his DEEPER mind shall bring forth.

At this point the student may ask, "How can this be, that man's SURFACE mind corresponds to Spirit? Spirit is sinless, without spot or blemish, always resting in perfect peace. Man's SURFACE mind is wicked, often devilish. I can't see this."

There is no contradiction here at all. Man is made in the image and likeness of God IN THAT HE POSSESSES THE QUALITIES, TRAITS, AND ABILITIES THAT ENABLE HIM TO CREATE HIS OWN WORLD BY THE SAME PROCESS THAT CREATED THE UNIVERSE. His SURFACE mind corresponds to Spirit in its power to *select* and to *initiate*.

MAN'S GREATEST ABILITY IS TO CHOOSE

Psychologists tell us that a characteristic of DEEPER mind is to accept and to obey any pattern set before it, and that man's conscious or SURFACE mind is characterized by selection and initiative. It is not so much the QUALITY of man's thinking but the ABILITY to select a certain course of action and to initiate the movement which fulfills it that makes man's SURFACE mind the counterpart of Spirit in the Originating Trinity. WE SHALL SEE LATER THAT THE POWER TO CHOOSE IS MAN'S GREATEST POWER.

SPIRIT HAS THE POWER OF
SELECTION AND INITIATIVE

Universal creation gives evidence of choice or selection by the fact that it is not universe-wide, but occurs in spots. What caused stars to be built at intervals? There is no scientific answer to this, but it is proof of the power of Spirit, the Originating Intelligence, to SELECT spots for creation; and so we can assume that one of the characteristics of Originating Intelligence is the power of SELECTION.

But there must be an additional power, for the ability to select without a concomitant power to carry out the choice would have left Spirit the prisoner of Its own imaginings. The very fact that creation was carried into form indicates, then, that Spirit has the power to select, then to initiate in Its Mind-phase the action that brings into manifestation that which Spirit has selected.

SIMILAR CHARACTERISTICS OF SPIRIT
AND SURFACE MIND

We continue to repeat that one of the fundamentals in the SCIENCE OF MIND is that man's SURFACE mind has the power of selection and initiative. But if this were all—if man had only the ability to select, and not the ability to initiate, he would be tantalized beyond endurance, always tormented by desire, yet without the power to attain. Fortunately, the Creative Process will work unfalteringly for man just as it did for Originating Intelligence. Each student can select a goal to be demonstrated before the completion of this course; he can then initiate the Creative Cycle by speaking his word, that is, by declaring its fulfillment, and he can go forward in the conviction that he can reach that goal—not in some far-off heaven beyond the grave, but here and now in his earth existence.

PROGRESS COMES FROM
USING THE POWER OF SELECTION

All man's advances have come through his power of choice. The rise from barbarism to civilization has been a repeated going on from one selection to a better one. But the power of selection has been exercised by comparatively few. The great masses, sunk in mental lethargy, have scarcely dreamed that there might be something higher and better. Thus they have been content with things as they have found them, things that their leaders have selected for them.

The thinkers of the race, filled with a "Divine discontent," have always chosen to seek the higher levels. In the material life, our inventors have selected the better way of doing things, hence our advance from horseback to the automobile and airplane, from pounding a shirt with a block of wood in a running stream to our modern washing machine and laundromat; from smoke signals on a hilltop to radio. Without the twin abilities to select a better way and to make it come true, man today would still be living in a cave.

MAN'S CONCEPT OF GOD IS GROWING

In the mental and spiritual field man has had a *growing* conception of the Infinite. Daring souls have weighed the old, measured it against a new idea, selected the new, and have been killed for it. But later the masses have accepted the new idea, and because of it have moved a step nearer to clear understanding. The Twentieth Century view of God is no more like the cruel monster of the Dark Ages than the automobile is like the Roman chariot.

The most modern view of God is that of the SCIENCE OF MIND, which appeals both to reason and to spiritual insight; and since it so definitely brings healing to all discordant conditions, it is evidently nearer the truth than the earlier conceptions, for "by their fruits shall ye know them."

It is comfortable to stay in a rut; it takes mental effort to get out; and the masses have always been angry when asked to pull free of their settled ignorance. Yet someone must pioneer, and when he does, usually he is accused of "doing away with God." No one can do away with God. He is quite able to look after Himself. The only thing the exploring thinker does away with is a superstitious CONCEPT of GOD.

Much of the "Zeal for God" is only zeal for one's settled opinions. Truth is inexhaustible, and the SCIENCE OF MIND view is by no means the ultimate. Yet, a hundred years from now, when someone tries to lead the people of the Twentieth Century onward to a still clearer truth, which assuredly will be forthcoming, the "settled ones" will probably fight just as strenuously for this Twentieth Century teaching.

When the newer Truth dawns, it will be through the ability of someone to SELECT the greater in place of the lesser.

WHAT IS GOD'S WILL?

Millions of persons today believe that it is the "will of God" that they should endure illness, poverty, unhappiness. They resign themselves to it, because they don't know that they can select a better level of life and move onto it. You, the student, are among the pioneers who emphatically reject this belief about the will of God. This course will enable you to prove to yourself and to others who are not blinded by prejudice that God's will for man is Good. Just as all man's advances have been brought about by the cool, conscious, deliberate choice of a better way, so your advance comes through dropping old false beliefs, and definitely CHOOSING this emancipation.

SPIRIT IS CAUSE—
MIND IS THE CREATIVE MEDIUM

You will notice by the foregoing chart that Spirit is Cause. Everything good that ever comes into our life will originate in our SURFACE mind, but the action that brings it to pass will be that of the DEEPER mind. "Mind" on the chart represents the working phase of the Trinity. It carries within itself all the "know-how" of creation. It knows how to build a sun or a planet, a blade of grass or a redwood, a cell or a child. It knows how to restore perfect structure and function in a body. It knows how every successful business was ever built, and how any person ever drew love and companionship into his life. Its knowledge is absolutely without limit. It is omniscient; yet it is dedicated to the will of the SURFACE mind, and will carry out to completion ANY pattern SURFACE mind sets steadily before it; and it will do this easily, effortlessly.

Spirit decides what it wants done and, as it were, says, "Let there be," thus passing the action onto Mind which, having no choice, always obeys and carries out the order. But there is nothing inferior about the place Mind holds in Trinity. It is not a slave. It is simply the WORKING PHASE of the One God.

DOUBLE ACTION IN ONENESS

This not altogether perfect analogy might make the point clearer: An architect brings his plans to the master builder and says, "Follow these out." The builder, without the slightest sense of inferiority, takes them and complies with the directions. He knows that the architect specializes in the drawing of plans, but does no building. He, the builder, draws no plans but specializes in building. It is by the co-operation of these two that all the beautiful and massive structures in the world are erected. So God as Spirit and God as Mind, two yet One, acting separately, are working in closest harmony.

In like manner there is no division between man's SURFACE and his DEEPER mind. They work together. The SURFACE mind selects and presents the blueprint, while DEEPER mind fabricates the drawing into form and substance.

GENESIS DESCRIBES THE CREATIVE PROCESS

The Old Testament story of creation may seem crude and naive, because it was set down in a day long before scientific findings in this field; yet it is remarkable how those ancient seers "felt" their way to scientific truths, and stated them in terms whose significance they probably did not fully grasp. When they wrote, "And God said, Let there be light: and there was light," they were describing this Creative Cycle—Spirit selecting and initiating the movement through the spoken word "Let there be," Mind obeying, swinging into action, applying its "know-how." "And there was light." It should be apparent now that the SCIENCE OF MIND does not depart from the Bible but reinterprets it in the light of modern knowledge.

Suppose we approach it from the following point of view: ORIG-INATING SPIRIT selects, decides, or intends to create the universe.

As part of Its Nature and Being, It has MIND the Builder, and BODY the Building Materials. These THREE ARE ONE, having always been present. Neither one has created the other two. There is an equality of nature and existence, but a division of function for some as yet unknown reason. (Perhaps it is because this is the way WE SEE its operation, there being no real division, but only an APPARENT division of function.)

The activity is thus seen in the following sequence: (1) SPIRIT SELECTS the object of creation and INITIATES the Creative Cycle by saying, "Let there be." (2) MIND, the Fabricator, obediently takes the decree and proceeds to carry it out to the most exact degree, as though following a blueprint. (3) MIND works upon BODY, the Unformed Primary Substance of the universe, which also has been present with Spirit and Mind from the beginning of beginnings—if there ever were a beginning—building solid form out of insubstantial matter.

For emphasis we repeat that Spirit's thought does not INFLU-ENCE the body—it actually BECOMES the body. Spirit creates a thing by becoming it. By lowering that which Spirit has selected (invisible) to a visible level (form) MIND completes the Creative Cycle.

Therefore, since both FORCE and SUBSTANCE were present from the beginning, coequal parts of the Originating Intelligence, the entire universe, including us, is the BODY of God. "It is the same God which worketh all in all." (I Cor. 12:6) "In Him we live and move and have our being." (Acts 17:28).

WHY ILLNESS DEVELOPS IN MAN

Perhaps the student is now coming to see that sickness and other misfortunes develop in man because DEEPER mind is compelled to accept whatever thoughts are given it. It has no power of choice at all. It is an automatic receptor of the choice already made by SURFACE mind. Whether it is constructive or destructive, DEEPER mind must carry out into form the thought of SURFACE mind. The person who is always thinking, talking, or reading about symptoms and illness is actually saying, "Let there be sickness."

That person will indignantly deny this, of course, but that doesn't change the fact that with his mouth he may be pleading for health, but with his thought he is ordering illness. We are not always aware of the quality of our thought, and certainly do not notice the lightning speed of our choices. Once we have become habituated to negative thought, we automatically choose this kind, then believe IT has forced itself upon us.

SURFACE MIND MUST SELECT
POSITIVE THOUGHTS

Every thought has two sides—the positive and the negative. Whenever a thought presents its discouraging side to us, we may know that its positive side is there also, waiting to be selected. For example, one cannot think of sorrow without also thinking of joy, because sorrow is the absence of joy. Illness is the absence of health. Poverty is the absence of prosperity. Failure is the absence of success. We can see now how highly important is this matter of selection.

Man's DEEPER mind is the seat of his emotions, his feelings. His SURFACE mind is the seat of his reason, his choices; and neither can carry on the activities of the other. They remain forever separate and distinct to our human eyes.

DEEPER mind depends on SURFACE mind to protect it from error; but after the same choice has been made repeatedly, DEEPER mind comes to expect that sort of choice to be made; and once the thought has passed into its sphere, it goes to work on it, fabricating it into form. Thus negativity or positivity is nothing but a mental habit to which DEEPER mind has become accustomed and automatically expresses. The encouraging feature of this is that DEEPER mind is highly educable; it CAN be re-educated.

Through repeated choice, a certain type of thought becomes a feeling. The person who lives by his feelings alone can never control the Creative Cycle, because he is allowing the servant to become the master. DEEPER mind must always remain the servant of SURFACE mind.

REASON AND CHOICE MUST
CONTROL THE FEELINGS

The mark of the civilized man is his ability to let reason and choice, and not feelings, prevail. There are three classes of persons who live by their feelings, or allow their feelings to dictate their actions. They are the savage, the child, and the insane—all unstable, undeveloped types. The person who says, "I just don't FEEL like working today," and who acts on that feeling, is headed for failure. His mentally developed brother will say, "I don't feel like working today, but I simply MUST get to work." This man is using choice and initiative, and is thus setting in action the Creative Cycle for a definite purpose. By the end of the day he will have produced something worthwhile.

ON WAKING UP "BLUE"

We often hear someone say, "I really intend to start thinking and acting positively; but when I wake in the morning, it seems as if a wave of gloom sweeps over me. I just can't get started." Many people often feel this way, but, while we cannot help it if the birds fly over our house, we CAN keep them from building nests in the eaves; and the way to do this is through selection and initiative. The first thing upon awakening, choose to slant the mind in the direction of the good. The slanting may be done in many ways. One student has found it helpful to say, "I wonder what nice experience I'll have today, what pleasant people I'll meet, what good business I'll do, what nice contacts I'll make." It has revolutionized her life.

DEEPER MIND CAN BE RE-EDUCATED

Cultivate the expectancy of good, and DO IT DELIBERATELY. If a myriad choices of the bad have gradually slanted the mind into a negative pattern, BEGIN AT ONCE to establish a new positive pattern. And remember, that even though one has thought negatively for forty years, it does not take forty years to overcome that habit. One constructive thought is more powerful than ten thousand destructive thoughts, because constructive thought is in line with the thinking of the Originating Intelligence and, therefore, has superlative force.

Start the next seven mornings in this way. It will pay real dividends, for you will find that you are on your way to a life in which your feelings will come to back up your CHOICES, not to determine them.

Thus we can change from bad thought habits to good ones, from a pessimistic disposition to an optimistic one. And once we begin to take this way of the creative process in the individual, we can make ourselves ANYTHING WE WANT TO BE.

The next lesson will deal with BODY, the third phase of the Trinity.

In another lesson we shall learn how to release our selections to the loom of mind in a way that ensures their being woven into the pattern of our lives.

SPECIAL HELPS IN STUDYING THE LESSON

These study-helps have been carefully prepared to help you get the most out of this course.

QUESTIONS

Educators have found that a series of questions enables the student to get a complete picture of the material studied. You will find the questions accompanying each lesson highly valuable in uncovering concepts which you might otherwise pass by.

We advise that you first study the lesson carefully, then put it aside, write the answers to the questions, and, finally, *check your answers by the lesson.*

Keep the answers as a running commentary on the course *for your own benefit.* At its conclusion you will find that they have become a record of your own growth in consciousness.

1. What must have been the source of the energy which created the universe?

2. Name the three aspects of the Trinity and the chief characteristics of each.

3. Explain, "Man is in the small that which God is in the large."

4. Exactly what is meant by the characteristics of selection and initiative?

5. What is the explanation for illness and other unwanted conditions in one's life?

WRITING SUGGESTION

Make at least seven positive statements that you can use this week to turn your thoughts in the right direction when you find them dwelling on things that you do not want in your life.

READING SUGGESTIONS

It is not imperative that the student read the books suggested for collateral reading, but we strongly recommend that he do so for deeper insight into the subject treated.

The books suggested may be available in your public library. If not, they may be purchased from our Book Department. Please consult our *Book Catalogue*.

Frederick Bailes, "What Is This Power That Heals?" and
Your Mind Can Heal You, Chs. III and VI
Thomas Troward, *The Creative Process in the Individual*, Ch. II

THOUGHT-TRAINING FOR THE WEEK

Follow the suggestion on page 14 of the lesson each morning this week. Decide that immediately on awakening you will deliberately turn your thought toward the good.

A DAILY THOUGHT

Let this thought be your daily thought during the week that you study this lesson.

I am an extension of Infinite Mind, and everything that
is true of that Mind must also be true of me.

A DAILY SELF-TREATMENT
(To be spoken quietly and thoughtfully each morning and evening)

"This day I seek a deeper understanding of myself. I know that I am part of the Infinite Intelligence. It is ageless; therefore, I know that the eternal currents of tireless energy flow through very cell of my body this day.

"It is perfect; therefore, there is no room in me for that which is called illness. It is Life; therefore, nothing destructive can operate to my hurt. It is Wisdom; therefore, my thought has balance so that I am guided in all right action this day. It is fullness; therefore, my cup of blessing overflows.

"This day I remain alive to my true nature, the visible expression of that Eternal Good which is forever invisible, which worketh in me to will and to do of its good pleasure."

SCIENCE OF MIND

Home-Study Extension Course

(copyright 1951)

by

DR. FREDERICK BAILES

LESSON V

THE CREATIVE PROCESS IN THE UNIVERSE AND IN THE INDIVIDUAL

In our previous lesson, we discussed the chart illustrating Troward's Creative Process, the three phases of the nature of the Originating Intelligence, and, incidentally, the nature and powers of man. Now, we move to the third segment of the circle, marked BODY.

BODY IS CHARACTERIZED BY INERTIA

The student should study the evidence until he is convinced that the Body of God refers to the entire visible universe; likewise that the body of man refers to his physical frame, his home, work, and other material interests. These constitute his world of effect. The outstanding characteristic of BODY is INERTIA. It is highly important to understand that all things which come under the term BODY, as here used, are characterized by INERTIA. This means that body cannot originate any movement from and of itself. It never acts upon anything, BUT IS ALWAYS ACTED UPON BY SOMETHING OUTSIDE OF ITSELF.

In the original Creative Cycle, SUBSTANCE (or BODY) was without form, and void. It was real, but intangible. It is the plastic, moldable material from which everything is formed into what is called matter. When we think of bodily healing, it is imperative that we remember that Substance has no power to resist being molded into form, because this is exactly what does happen during a healing. Man's physical body is substance. During a healing, the old form passes away; a new form is created under the activity of Mind.

In the original Creative Cycle, we saw that Body, or Substance, was present with Spirit and Mind, but did not take the form of a universe until selection and initiative had operated upon it to set the design. Once the design is set, Body, of itself, CANNOT alter it. It can only be altered by force applied to it from outside itself. From this it can be seen that the shaping of the body is determined by the energy called thought.

Thought is the molder of the body.

BODY IS OPERATED UPON BY THOUGHT

It is quite evident, then, that man's body, of itself, being characterized by INERTIA, can neither produce nor heal a disease, nor make any other change within itself. It is forever played upon by the images of man's thought. Separated from mind, it can do nothing. (Look up the word INERTIA in a dictionary.)

The arm moves because mind tells it to move. Severed from the body in which the mind operates, it cannot move. It will lie inert until it slowly disintegrates unless some force outside itself acts upon it. A foot can kick it; the table on which it lies may be shaken; a strong wind may blow against it—these outside forces can move it. But of itself, it cannot move because of its inherent inertia. In this it is like any other piece of inert matter—a rock, for instance, which will stay where it is unless some outside force moves it.

In similar manner, the severed arm could not develop a disease, as can the arm on a living person. In order to become diseased, the arm must be attached to a body through which mind operates. (Disintegration is not disease; it is a perfectly natural process by which everything reverts to its original elements after it has performed its useful function and is no longer needed.)

ILLNESS BEGINS IN THE THOUGHT

BODY IS ALWAYS ACTED UPON. Man's brain is a dynamo of power. Here are generated those currents of nerve energy which flow over the vast and intricate network of nerves to every part of the body. Each individual cell is indwelt by intelligence, but the intelligence is not of itself; a cell separated from the body shows no intelligent action. THE INTELLIGENCE OF THE CELL IS THE INTELLIGENCE OF THE PERSON OF WHOM THE CELL IS A PART.

Wave after wave of thought flows from the brain every moment we live. The thought is of either a constructive or a destructive nature. It colors every cell through which it passes, imparting its own quality to the cell. Thus the person whose dominant strain of thought is that of anxiety, inward pressure, and irritation will eventually find the tissues of his body showing these patterns. In most instances it shows up in the stomach cells, which seem more easily irritated than those of other organs. That irritation, if allowed to continue unchanged, can show up as gastritis, which is irritation of the stomach lining. If this is not sufficient to cause the person to change his thought patterns, it can eventuate as stomach ulcers.

CHANGED THOUGHT PRODUCES
CHANGED CONDITIONS

It is well known that the physical means for dealing with ulcers have not been highly successful. Surgery has been done in which that portion of the stomach involved has been excised; yet in a few years many such patients have been back for more surgery. All the surgeon's knife had done was remove the effect; the cause of the ulcers had been left untouched. Various bland diets produce only temporary relief; when they are discontinued, the ulcers come back, because, as in the surgical cases, the cause has not yet been dealt with.

On the other hand, there are thousands of cases on record in which, without either surgery or diet, ulcer patients have been completely restored to health through a changed mental and emotional attitude.

Sufferers say, "I could be happy if it were not for my stomach." The fact is, the stomach could be happy if it were not for the person. The cells of the body really enjoy ease, not dis-ease. We might become facetious for a moment and picture two stomach cells talking together. The one says, "I wish that fellow upstairs would stop being mad at everybody. I'm burning up down here." The other replies, "Yes, and he's the one who's always telling his friends what a burden WE are to HIM!"

TO MIND THERE ARE NO
INCURABLE DISEASES

Because of this principle of inertia, THERE ARE NO INCUR-ABLE DISEASES. Body will readily move in any direction in which the mental currents are directed. But since people don't know this, sickness reigns and the sufferers blaspheme God by saying that He, for some inscrutable reason, imposes disease upon them. GOD NEVER LAYS SICKNESS UPON ANYONE. Man brings it upon himself, and he can get rid of it as soon as he is willing to deal with it intelligently.

The writer of this course was condemned to die of diabetes in 1915. Today, he is in better health than he was in his youth, because he has learned that the body is the sounding board of the mind, and that man's mental attitudes BECOME his physical tissues. Insulin had not been discovered in 1915, or he assuredly would have begun taking it; for he was medically minded then, having just finished his training in London Missionary School of Medicine and London Homeopathic Hospital for what was then to have been his life work as a medical missionary. Had insulin been available at that time, it is highly probable that this course and many books on the SCIENCE OF MIND would never have been written, and the progress of this truth would have been delayed by that much, at least.

As encouragement to anyone who has not had immediate results from his changed viewpoint, may we point out that it took more than four years before the writer was entirely sugar-free. He COULD have been healed instantaneously had his understanding been complete, but in the beginning he knew nothing at all of the SCIENCE OF MIND; and the Infinite can do FOR us only that which It can do THROUGH us at any stage of our unfoldment.

WHY SOME CONDITIONS SEEM INCURABLE

The body cannot refuse the dictates of Spirit even if it wanted to, which it certainly does not. Man has been deluded in the past because certain diseases have been labeled "curable" and others "incurable." To DEEPER mind, nothing is incurable; and it knows no such terms as hard and easy, big and little, serious and simple. One gets a pimple on the nose, laughs at it, and says, "It will be gone in a day or two." One day we hope we shall come to the place where we can say the same thing of a cancer, knowing it will be healed.

Of course we know that, from today's human and scientific point of view, the destructive processes at work in a cancer are far more deadly than those in a pimple. Furthermore, they are not at all the same processes. But we must remember when we give spiritual treatment to those conditions, that we are dealing with a Power that is Omniscient and Omnipotent. Remember, also, that while human research has not yet uncovered a sure-fire method of treating cancer, malignancies have been healed from time to time through spiritual means ever since the day Jesus healed the woman with the "running sore." In these cases, human skill was by-passed, and the Great Physician called in. When "That-to-Which-Nothing-Is-Hidden" went to work, healing was the result.

Then why are not all cancers healed? Because the human mind has been conditioned to the belief that some are incurable. None of us is aware of the race beliefs he carries in his DEEPER mind and of their intensity. But here and there is a person who breaks through the shell of the race thought and emerges into the clear light of Infinite Mind. When he does, the healing follows.

CONSCIOUSNESS IS THE KEY TO HEALING

It is natural that the student should be eager to learn the actual techniques of treatment. We have not yet gone into them at any length, because the broad foundation we are endeavoring to lay is that of CONSCIOUSNESS.

A high healing consciousness coupled with imperfect technique will produce more healings than a perfect knowledge of techniques without the healing consciousness. The medical profession has sometimes been amazed when an unlettered person, perhaps one whose speech is atrociously ungrammatical, and who knows nothing of anatomy or physiology, has been able to produce sensational healings. The secret is CONSCIOUSNESS.

The healing consciousness is not a gift vouchsafed to some fortunate persons. Anyone can cultivate it. It grows out of much thinking upon the bigness of the universe, the Wisdom and Power that guides the stars and planets, the Life that works such beautiful veinings into the tiniest flower and puts the fragrance into the rose.

CONSCIOUSNESS OF GOODNESS

It grows out of a belief in the essential goodness of human nature even when the acts of individuals are vile, and of a universal quality of love for all men. This latter is perhaps its most important ingredient.

CONSCIOUSNESS OF BEAUTY

It is that in man which is enthralled by the rare beauty of a sunset, but which does not stop at the aesthetic satisfaction of it, but goes further into a contemplation of Absolute Beauty, of which the sunset is only a tiny scintilla.

CONSCIOUSNESS OF INFINITY

It is that in man which, when he sits on a headland overlooking the vastness of the ocean, watching the steady rolling of waves as they tumble ashore, leads his thoughts on to that Infinite Ocean of Mind, of which his mind is a part, the Ocean of Mind that is powerful enough to sweep away the towering cliff of cancer as easily as it wipes out the sand-pile of a pimple.

CONCIOUSNESS OF LOVE

The healing consciousness in man is that which knows that the highest expression of love he has ever seen—whether it be devotion between husband and wife, devotion of a mother for her spastic child, or devotion to country which sends young men to death with a smile on their lips—is only the faintest adumbration of some phase of Infinite

Love. And since a river can rise no higher than its source, it also knows that if such heights of love are possible in earthly beings, then beyond and behind such human love there must be an Infinite Love without limit.

The healing consciousness is many more things, but these mentioned may faintly indicate the difference between acquired knowledge and consciousness. Later in the course we shall go further into the subject.

CONSCIOUSNESS OF HARMONY

This course is being prepared at a beautiful spot high in the mountains of California, in the shade of a huge oak which has evidently seen the suns and snows of more than two hundred years, and from whose shade I have sped my healing thought to thousands of men and women. In the clean air is that quiet, lulling hum of mountains drowsing in the sun. As my nearest neighbor is almost half a mile away, there isn't a house nor any other sign of human being in sight.

A black and white retriever, which has adopted me, has followed me here and lies stretched at my feet in perfect relaxation. I hear the soft chatter of a squirrel, which has climbed the oak, and is looking down at me in friendly inquiry.

Birds in the surrounding trees are singing. Redheaded woodpeckers are bathing in the bird bath close by, and between times enjoying the bread crusts I have tossed there for them.

Scores of butterflies — yellow, cinnamon-brown, or white — flit about on their mysterious quests. And just now a flying insect, whose name I do not know, has made a landing on the rough board which is my desk. He is not more than three-fourths of an inch long, brown, and shaped exactly like a prehistoric Brontosaurus, with a long, outthrust neck, small snake-like head, and light-brown wings folded easily at his sides. He stays motionless, seemingly looking me over. He has no fear of me, even when I move my finger close to him. But presently, as if his curiosity has been satisfied, he spreads his wings and flies away.

In these beautiful, natural surroundings, particularly at this peaceful moment when no creature seems to be afraid of any other creature, I feel one with the harmony of nature. And I can well understand that harmony is a part of the nature of God. Seeking an analogy in music, I might say that all this is like a grand symphony to which many different instruments have contributed, each one blending its special sound and appearance with the others to make up a harmonious whole.

It is not difficult, now, to move my thought on to harmony in the human body, which, as God fashioned it, is an expression of Divine Harmony. This body is made up of many different parts, each with its particular function to perform, each actively looking out for itself, yet all functioning together for the good of the whole.

All this is the CONSCIOUSNESS of harmony; yet it is but the tiniest fragment of something far more vast that extends to the limits of the universe and beyond; for our universe has no limits, because it is the Body of God.

These are some ways in which students keep alive their high healing consciousness. No matter where one lives, there is always some secluded spot not far distant where he can be "alone with God," insulated from the bombardment of the world's thought. Even if he can get there only once a week, it will prove invaluable.

TREATMENT IS NEVER A PETITIONING PRAYER

Now, let us return to the chart in Lesson IV illustrating Troward's Creative Process. You will notice that it states that Spirit is never acted upon. This is true; and it is the reason that we, in the SCIENCE OF MIND, DO NOT use petition in our prayers. We never say, "Dear God, look upon this misery and get me (or this other person) out of it." Instead of petitioning, we declare the TRUTH about ourselves or the other person, believing that IT IS THE TRUTH THAT SETS ONE FREE.

One of the ancient writers said that God is "of purer eyes than to behold evil, and cannot look upon iniquity." (Hab. 1:13) That means that the universe must look entirely different to Infinite Spirit from what it looks to us. We, newcomers in it, see imperfections. Spirit, the Originator, sees it perfect as He made it.

ALL CREATION IS THE
SELF-CONTEMPLATION OF SPIRIT

Troward makes much of the fact that the Originating Spirit creates by self-contemplation, and that, since there is only one Creative Process, man creates in the same way, whether he knows it or not.

After picturing the Originating Source, the Three-in-One, Troward develops the idea that, since there was nothing else out of which a universe could have been constructed—there being only God and nothing—the only way in which things could have taken form must have been through the Originating Being thinking of Himself as being projected AS the various forms in the universe.

It is notable that the world-famous physicist, Sir James Jeans, comes to the same conclusion. Jeans had gone into a search for the way in which this universe could have come into being. After having exhausted every possible hypothesis, he says:

> The universe can best be pictured as consisting of pure thought, the thought of what for want of a better word we must describe as a mathematical thinker. (Sir James Jeans, Rede Memorial Lectures, Cambridge, 4 Nov. 1930)

Since BODY was part of God, as shown in the previous lessons, it is evident that the universe would have to be produced out of THAT part of Himself; therefore, God saw Himself projected in form, AS a universe, when he foresaw a universe spun out of the Universal Primary Substance. So creation is the act of Spirit contemplating Itself in a certain form or state of being. Mind, always obedient, then fabricated the universe in accordance with Spirit's thought-pattern, and the Creative Process, or Cycle, was completed.

Since Body was a part of the Trinity of Spirit, it is quite conceivable that Spirit THOUGHT of this other part of Itself as being projected from Itself in the various forms we now see. Science has no other satisfactory explanation. God, SEEING HIMSELF as a certain thing, thereby BECOMES that thing, and that which Spirit sees is always the Good. It is interesting to note how the writer of Genesis "feels" his way to a similar conclusion. He says, "And God saw everything that he had made, and behold, it was very good." (Gen. 1:31)

Man as spirit (SURFACE mind) likewise creates by self-contemplation. "As a man thinketh in his heart, so is he." (Prov. 23:7) Whatever man is conscious of being, he becomes, for Mind, always obedient, fabricates his thought into the stuff of his affairs. If one's most vivid self-contemplation is of his illness, Mind cannot fabricate health. If of his poverty or loneliness, Mind cannot fabricate prosperity or companionship. Luck or favoritism do not enter in; it is the inexorable working of Cause and Effect.

SPIRIT SEES PERFECTION; MAN SEES IMPERFECTION

Spirit, then, always sees things as they really are—perfect. That is why Spirit is never acted upon by man. Man, seeing through the warped vision of the senses, beholds illness, grief, misery in the very same place where Spirit sees Itself in perfect form. This is why our statement "There is nothing to heal," is so difficult for some people to understand. What we mean is this: The only thing to heal is the false belief, for all is Spirit in form; therefore, all is good, all is perfect.

It is man's perspective as regards the universe that makes him doubt this. It is somewhat similar to that which we have had in the old-time motion picture theaters. Seated down front and off to the far side, we saw the actors on the screen all out of perspective: long pipestems for legs, long narrow heads. If that were all we had ever known about motion pictures, we never should have gone back again. But someone takes us to the center of the theater or, better still, up into the operator's booth, from which the images are thrown on the screen; then we see the images as they really are.

In the present stage of his development, man finds himself sitting away off to the side. If he could, as it were, step up and look over God's shoulder, he would see things as they actually are; then he would know why we say, "There is nothing to heal except a belief."

PURPOSE OF TREATMENT—
TO HEAL THE FALSE BELIEF

Treatment is for the purpose of bringing our thought "up into the operator's booth" to heal our false belief of distortion. This is why we so often say that we do not treat the body as such; we treat the underlying belief. The student must get this important point clear in his mind; otherwise he will find himself treating EFFECTS rather than CAUSES.

When a condition is intelligently treated and healed through spiritual methods, it can never return, because the false belief that supported it has been destroyed.

If the treated condition is removed only temporarily, it is a sign that our treatment has been only on the psychological level, or the level of suggestion or hypnosis. Many of the conditions removed through psychological treatment return. The reason is this: the conditions were healed by the MIND OF THE PSYCHOLOGIST, and when his mind let go of the patient, there was a recurrence; whereas, when we come to the lesson on treatment, we shall see that we form the picture; then we RELEASE it to the Infinite Mind, which never slumbers nor sleeps, and which holds it to the end of the Creative Cycle.

Now the student can see why a person's whole manner of life enters into his treatment. It is because our life is an expression of our deepest beliefs. Our unexpressed beliefs color our consciousness. To heal the body or the business, one must heal the belief. To heal the belief, one must understand the importance of selection and initiative and their place in the creative cycle.

a. First, the intelligence selecting;
b. then, the intelligence initiating the cycle by "Let there be";
c. then, the action passing over into Mind, which does the work and which then
d. moves upon body, through Law, to follow the pattern selected.
e. Body, thus acted upon, is molded into the desired form.

ALL THIS GROWS OUT OF A CHANGED BELIEF.

SPECIAL HELPS FOR STUDYING THE LESSON

These study-helps have been carefully prepared to help you get the most out of this course.

QUESTIONS

Educators have found that a series of questions enables the student to get a complete picture of the material studied. You will find the questions accompanying each lesson highly valuable in uncovering concepts which you might otherwise pass by.

We advise that you first study the lesson carefully, then put it aside, write the answers to the questions, and, finally, *check your answers by the lesson.*

Keep the answers as a running commentary on the course *for your own benefit.* At its conclusion you will find that they have become a record of your own growth in consciousness.

1. What is the chief characteristic of body and what is the great significance of this truth?

2. When results are not forthcoming when we think they should be, what attitude should we take?

3. How can one proceed definitely to cultivate a healing consciousness?

4. How does knowing that *Spirit is never acted upon* affect the way in which we pray?

5. What is the underlying difference between psychological treatment and spiritual treatment?

WRITING SUGGESTION

Write your own version of "The Universe Is a Grand Symphony" or "Harmony Is the Keynote of the Universe."

READING SUGGESTIONS

It is not imperative that the student read the books suggested for collateral reading, but we strongly recommend that he do so for deeper insight into the subjects treated.

The books suggested may be available in your public library. If not, they may be purchased from our Book Department. Please consult our *Book Catalogue*.

Frederick Bailes, "Healing the 'Incurable' "
Your Mind Can Heal You, Ch. VI
Thomas Troward, *The Creative Process in the Individual*, Ch. II

THOUGHT-TRAINING FOR THE WEEK

Raise your consciousness of healing by meditating on the activities and manifestations of the Infinite mentioned beginning at the bottom of page 5 and extending through page 6.

A DAILY THOUGHT

Let this thought be your daily thought during the week that you study this lesson:

The healing process in man knows no limit except that placed upon it by our timidity, blindness, selfishness, or resentments.

A DAILY SELF-TREATMENT
(To be spoken quietly and thoughtfully each morning and evening)

"This day I stand at the door of limitless opportunity. Life beckons to me and smiles encouragement. Life flows through me, touching my body with its Infinite Healing Presence and blotting out everything unlike itself. Life pours itself through my business this day bringing increase of opportunity to serve and to be recompensed.

"My home and my loved ones are blessed this day and surrounded by right action. Peace, health, and happiness rule all my affairs this day, this week, this month. I release my word to the Infinite Mind and relax in the knowledge that IT IS SO."

SCIENCE OF MIND

Home-Study Extension Course

(copyright 1951)

by

DR. FREDERICK BAILES

LESSON VI

THE SENSE OF AUTHORITY

One of the tendencies of modern science is to spiritualize matter. A modern scientist would say that matter is composed of force, expressed as electrons—positive and negative charges of electricity. In the metaphysical field we use other words to say the same thing: namely, that matter is Spiritual Substance, or the Substance of Spirit. Our bodies are Spiritual Substance condensed into form; but, man, of course, being in the small what God is in the large, is more than body. He also is mind and he is spirit.

THE FOUNDATION FOR AUTHORITY

In the two preceding lessons we discussed the Trinity—the three phases of the One God, namely:

Spirit—which, by thought, selects, initiates, and says, "Let there be."

Mind—which always obeys and knows how to bring into manifestation the desire of Spirit—and does so.

Body—which is the inert Spiritual (or Primary) Substance upon which Mind acts, condensing It into the form of the thing which Spirit has selected and decreed.

This sums up the one Creative Process, as set forth by Troward, the process used by God to create the universe, which is His Body; it is likewise the process used by man, whether he is aware of it or not, to create HIS world, including the condition of his material body and all his circumstances and affairs.

We have seen that the paramount thing in this Creative Process is THOUGHT. We shall now see further how this applies to the healing of the body.

THOUGHT ACTUALLY BECOMES FORM

It must be remembered that thought does not only influence form —IT ACTUALLY BECOMES FORM.

To the average student this is something that will need explanation. "How," he will ask, "can dense matter emerge from immaterial thought? How can anything as solid as rock, for instance, be composed of the same substance as thought—the finer vibration of Spirit?"

Troward developed the argument that the whole creation was drawn out of Originating Spirit. If that is so, then in some way it MUST HAVE already been present, hidden within Spirit.

We could use the illustration of the three-segmented telescope. At first sight it appears to be a single cylinder, but we pull out the second segment, then the third, both of which are part of its structure. This might appear astounding to a savage, seeing it for the first time. It is only three-in-one, as he soon learns.

For the purpose of instruction, we may think of Spirit as being like the first seen cylinder, then Mind emerging as the fabricator, finally form (Body) being brought into view. The illustration is reluctantly used since it does not fully illustrate the Creative Cycle, except from the standpoint of appearance.

We might also repeat this homely illustration from an earlier lesson. We know that true steam is invisible. That which we see a short distance from the kettle spout is a visible lowered condensation of the invisible steam emerging right at the spout. Lower its molecular vibration further by passing it through or over condenser coils, and this invisible steam will show up as water. Lower it still further in condensation by freezing, and it becomes hard, solid ice. All these different forms, from invisible steam to hard, solid ice, are due to changes in the vibration of the same substance brought about by the operation of a natural law.

And it is by operation of creative law that THOUGHT, invisible and intangible, BECOMES THE BODY OF MAN.

MAN'S BODY IS THOUGHT-ENERGY IN FORM

We say, then, that the body is a living thing composed of thought. Some of our scientists have called this universe itself "a living Presence" and have argued that every cell and atom is alive in a certain way.

If a person continues to think of his body as a hard, solid object, it is understandable that his consciousness of healing it through thought will never be very strong. To dispel such an illusion, we shall take up the question from another angle.

Every moment man lives, he is rebuilding new cells to take the place of those which are momentarily wearing out. It has been estimated that man builds at least TEN MILLION CELLS EVERY SECOND THAT HE LIVES. And every single cell is built under either a negative thought-pattern or a positive thought-pattern; for as the thought of the Originating Intelligence, falling into form, BECAME the universe, so man's thought, falling into form, becomes his body. Thus it is not a question of man's intangible weak thought bombarding his hard flesh in an endeavor to change it; it is a matter of man's selecting the highest grade of health-thought possible, so that this, falling into form, will become a healthy body.

There is no such thing as a chronic disease, BUT THERE ARE MANY CHRONIC (DISEASE) THINKERS. And this is the reason: Some authorities say that the entire body is built anew every seven to fourteen months, although this is disputed by others, who say that the elements merely shift from one tissue to another. It can be seen that in a sick person, a diseased cell must go to make room for a new cell. What, then, creates a new diseased cell to take the place of the worn-out one which has gone? A continuance of the old destructive thought-pattern. That is all!

Thus it can readily be seen that one big obstacle to healing is removed.

"But," says the self-doubting student, "I don't believe MY thought is powerful enough to heal. I'm not a trained thinker; my education has been too limited. In addition, my will-power is so weak I know I'd give up before my thought could influence my flesh."

When the student really comes to understand that the healing process does not involve his will-power or struggle, but that his thought BECOMES flesh, his consciousness of healing will be greatly strengthened.

The student will gain further assurance when he comes to know that the Infinite Mind flows steadily and continuously through his brain at all times, and that Infinite Mind carries the memory of a million healings. He is now dealing, not with human frailty, but with the ABSOLUTE POWER AND WISDOM—the Power and Wisdom that have never been balked or turned back, but have always accomplished their ends. We shall deal with this subject in more detail in a later lesson.

NEITHER SELF-DEPRECIATION NOR CONCEIT

There are two extremes of thought to which the student may go, and both will defeat his attempts to heal. We have already mentioned self-depreciation—the low estimate of one's mental ability to accomplish his ends. The other extreme is conceit (overwhelming self-esteem) which is evidence that the student has his mind on himself, rather than on the tremendous power of the Infinite. The person who says, "I am a powerful healer," has stepped out of the Divine placement. He who says, "This is a marvelous Law of Healing," will continue to heal.

JESUS WAS WELL-BALANCED

It is noticeable that Jesus avoided both these extremes. He was fully aware, always, that the remarkable healings attributed to him were not accomplished by the human Jesus of Nazareth, son of Mary, but by the *christos*, the Christ of God which indwelt him. When the people would have lionized him, he said, "Of myself I can do nothing. It is the Father in me who doeth the work."

Jesus also said, "I and the Father are one," because he knew that whatever God was in the large, he, Jesus, was in the small, and he knew that the selfsame power which brought the world into being was working through him to bring new bodies to those who gathered about him for healing. It was his complete sense of oneness with the Infinite and with the Infinite's method of creating, and not self-aggrandizement, which prompted his statement, "I and the Father are one."

MAN IS AN EXTENSION OF INFINITE MIND

It is evident that Jesus considered himself an extension of the Divine. He constantly kept his thinking in line with what he believed the eternal thinking to be; the oneness of which he spoke IS A ONE-NESS OF THOUGHT — the true oneness. And it was a practical oneness. It is the reason that Jesus never railed at his enemies and accusers and that he graciously forgave those who killed him. He knew that "No man taketh my life from me, but I lay it down of myself." (John 10:18) In all of this he was keeping himself in line with the Creative Process and making his view of things coincide with that of the Divine, of which he was an extension.

We said in an earlier lesson that man is an extension of the Divine as the inlet is an extension of the ocean. Analyze a drop of ocean water and one from an inlet and the same proportions of hydrogen and oxygen will be found in each. The inlet, though circumscribed by form, is still a part of the boundless ocean. In like manner, man, bounded by a body, is still a part of the Infinite, and is as eternal and indestructible. Man, "the drop," is in the small what God, "the ocean," is in the large.

WHATEVER IS TRUE OF INFINITE MIND IS TRUE OF MAN

Man is an extension of Infinite Mind; therefore, whatever is true of that Mind is true of him. THIS IS HIGHLY IMPORTANT.

Does the Infinite have power to transcend every obstacle that might be thrown against It? Then so do we.

Does It know that It can never be left stripped of Its resources, because there is always a steady flow of all that is necessary for the fulfilling of life? Then so do we.

Does It see always the beautiful and never the ugly? Then so can we.

Does It rest always in the quiet assurance of perfect peace and harmony? Then also can we.

Has the Infinite power to bring anything to pass, no matter how complex? Then we, also, have that selfsame power.

Does supply flow like an endless river through every phase of the Infinite? Then so does supply flow through all our affairs.

Does the Infinite rest forever in the contemplation of Beauty of outer and inner? Then our minds, too, can always be filled with "those things which are beautiful, noble, and of good report." (Phil. 4:8)

The fact is that man's TRUE nature is the nature of God. Whenever he experiences less than this, he is in fact believing an untruth. Thus, basically, man's troubles are the result of a FALSE BELIEF. True healing, then, is the healing of this false belief.

THE CONSCIOUSNESS OF ONENESS GIVES POWER

Since man's true nature is nothing but an extension of the Infinite, it can be readily seen that what is called oneness with God must be oneness of thinking: that is, man thinking God's thoughts after Him.

This Oneness of God and Man is not hypothetical. It is actual. Man derives strength from his unified consciousness, unified with Infinite Right Action. When the personality becomes disintegrated, it is because that person sees TWO things: that which he desires, which the Infinite also sees, and an obstructing power which can block him from the attainment of his desire, which Infinite Mind does not recognize. The psychologist uses the term "frustration" for this double vision, and it is well-known that frustrated persons are always unhappy persons who may become neurotic or worse.

Frustration will be unknown when man comes to understand that his true nature is divine, an inheritance from and an extension of the Infinite. From his physical antecedents he inherits his physical form and characteristics; these constitute his physical, or outer, nature. From the Divine he inherits a spotless Perfection, a life-giving Power, and and an eternal Wisdom which can make him anything he wants to become. These constitute his true spiritual, or inner, nature.

It is a sign of man's bondage to the negative that he persistently ties himself to his HUMAN heritage and becomes one with it instead of uniting with his DIVINE. Frequently, we hear someone discussing a "family weakness" and excusing himself by saying, "My mother (or father) was always like that; so I suppose I come by it honestly."

The fact of the matter is, man's divine qualities far outweigh his weak human heredity, and if he would continue to live as though he believed that "I and the Father are one," his human heritage would be very satisfactorily submerged.

TRANSCENDING THE PROBLEM
IS HIGHLY IMPORTANT

In facing a so-called family weakness or any other problem, there are three possible courses to pursue. They are: Fight, Flight, and Transcendence.

Some persons fight with all their might against unwanted conditions; they fight furiously against those who oppose them. Then there are those who seek refuge from trouble in flight. Especially will they do this when it comes to their own weaknesses; they will never face them, or do anything to remove them or to improve themselves.

Jesus did not fight nor run away. He calmly rose in consciousness to that place where he could say, "The prince of this world cometh, and findeth nothing [no response] in me." (John 14:30)

There is a level of living where one does not have to control his anger, for anger simply is not there. If, when another viciously opposes or attempts to obstruct us, we get down on his level and fight, we unify with him. Oneness with the Father means to live in a mental world so far above the sordid level of our opponent that there is no point of contact with him. Only that which finds response in us can attach itself to us, and if nothing within us vibrates on the plane of discord and violence, these pass us by. It was on the highest level that Jesus lived.

Of course, it is HUMAN nature (not divine) to want to get even with those who have wronged us—to "tell them off." And humans are inclined to attribute this reaction to righteous indignation rather than to what it really is—the lower self finding a satisfaction in retaliation, a satisfaction which is a very poor one. The highest satisfaction comes from knowing that "greater is he that is in you than he that is in the world." (1 John 4:4)

Each of us houses two tenants — a larger and a smaller self. The smaller one is the self magnified by the world in general. We, in the SCIENCE OF MIND, seek to magnify the larger self, and make that self "greater than he that is in the world."

Here, again, we exercise our power of selection. Man stands between his larger and smaller selves; he can hold out the hand to either the lesser or the greater self. When we choose the greater, we are meeting our problem by transcending it.

DESTRUCTIVE HABITS

We digress at this point to touch on something which will receive complete treatment later on—the victory over destructive habits gained through transcendence. The SCIENCE OF MIND way to free onself from a bad habit is not to fight it, but to lose all desire for it. There is a higher state of consciousness than desire to quit the habit, or desire to master it, or desire to continue it. That state above all desire connected with it is the state where one is so occupied with the reality of life, as it pertains to his own person, that everything less than the complete self does not exist. This is what we shall go into fully in later lessons.

The many people who think they are dealing with their problems by never asserting themselves are really only running away from them. There is the wife, for instance, who, in the presence of a bullying husband, will remain silent for fear of touching off a worse scene. And there is the person who becomes a doormat for employer or fellow employees, because he will not face the realities of a situation. These individuals give in when they should assert themselves.

It is one thing to give in from fear, and a totally different thing to refrain from forcing an issue because of a sense of mastery. The first is cowardice. The second is courage of the highest order. The latter was the sort of courage that gave Jesus his very positive attitude of authority.

THE AUTHORITY OF JESUS

In reading the life of Jesus, it is interesting to note how often the word "authority" was used concerning him. The people recognized a very real sense of authority in the way he spoke. He was not loud, not bombastic, not arrogant. He was courteous and considerate, with the serene assurance that comes from knowledge and an impregnable inner strength. It is written: "The people were astonished at his doctrine, for he taught them as one having authority, and not as the scribes." (Matt. 7:28-29, also Mark 1:22)

AUTHORITY COMES THROUGH "KNOWING"

There is a difference in the power of a man's word when he really knows what he is talking about. The salesman who knows his goods, and also knows his competitor's so well that, if challenged, he can give reasons why his are better—this man has an inward sense of authority which creates sales. The same thing is true of the speaker who really has had an experience of the truth he talks about.

The scribes and the Pharisees, all men of learning, were professional religionists, but they had never penetrated to the heart of Reality. They were learned in the things that they had been taught in schools, but Jesus had gone beyond mere book learning; he had gone off by himself and thought these things through, as you are doing now. He had penetrated into that quiet place in the unseen world where spirit with Spirit can meet; he had touched the Infinite, and grasped the underlying law that makes man's thought potent. He had come to KNOW certain things, not merely believe them. Thus he spoke with authority.

It is said of Jesus that he acted with authority. Those who saw him cast out devils (insanity) and still the stormy waters of the lake were mystified by something beyond his mere words. They said that his was such a sense of authority that not only devils but the winds and waves obeyed him.

And in that final scene, where he stood before Pilate—perhaps the most dramatic scene in history—Jesus, the prisoner, imposed his authority on Pilate, the powerful procurator of Judea, to such an extent that the latter was glad to get rid of him. Jesus, the steady-eyed, composed prisoner, looked through Pilate, the nervous, uncertain judge, and both onlookers and participants in that scene knew whose was the real authority. Pilate had that of the Roman Empire, and was able to sentence the prisoner to physical death; Jesus had that of the Inner Kingdom, heaven, and knew he was able to rise above death.

HOW TO GAIN AUTHORITY IN TREATMENT

There must be no uncertainty in treatment. The student must develop, within himself, such a clear concept of what goes on during a treatment that he has not the slightest doubt but that the manifestation will come. The prayers of many are nothing but an expression of their FEARS; therefore, they are not answered. The student's treatment must be a statement of his BELIEFS and of his KNOWING, because KNOWING is higher than BELIEVING.

He must know that when he treats, something begins to happen on the hidden side of life that was not happening before he treated. He must come into a sure and certain knowledge of the fact that "my word shall not return unto me void, but it shall accomplish that which I please, and it shall prosper in the thing whereto I sent it." (Isa. 55:11) He can gain this certainty by becoming thoroughly familiar with the following two facts:

1. The complete obedience of his DEEPER mind.
2. The readiness of the loom of mind to carry through into form those thoughts he feeds into it.

The beginning of a real sense of authority is to know that the Law of Mind is as obedient as the law of electricity. To know also that the working of the Law does not depend on the student's "goodness" or "badness," or his weakness or his strength lays a still firmer foundation for that inner sense of quiet authority which we feel sure he will acquire before he completes this course.

CULTIVATE CONSCIOUSNESS
ABOVE TECHNIQUES

It is hoped that the student has now come to see the very great importance of CONSCIOUSNESS. Techniques can always be learned; CONSCIOUSNESS is a matter of growth in the cultivation of certain inward attitudes.

Thousands of salesmen are buying courses in salesmanship and wondering why their study of these does not lead them to produce a greater volume of sales. These courses teach the externals—the way to approach the prospect, how to arouse his interest, how to guide the interview toward a decision, and, at last, how to close the deal. But the big thing, that inner attitude which is, as it were, the gasoline that drives the engine, is too often missing.

I once taught the Long Beach (California) Realty Board a course in salesmanship. At the beginning, I explained that I was not going to teach them the mechanics of selling; they had completed several courses which had taught them that. I said I was going to try to impart to them those inner states of mind, the sales consciousness which would be the actual deciding elements in closing their sales.

At the conclusion of the lessons, I received a letter from the secretary of the Board saying that the men had agreed my course was better than all the other courses they had taken, and that, as a result of taking it, EVERY member of that class had reported not only larger sales but, also, CLEANER sales.

Cultivate your inner CONSCIOUSNESS.

Our next lesson will go into the technique of treatment.

SPECIAL HELPS IN STUDYING THE LESSON

These study-helps have been carefully prepared to help you get the most out of this course.

QUESTIONS

Educators have found that a series of questions enables the student to get a complete picture of the material studied. You will find the questions accompanying each lesson highly valuable in uncovering concepts which you might otherwise pass by.

We advise that you first study the lesson carefully, then put it aside, write the answers to the questions, and, finally, *check your answers by the lesson*.

Keep the answers as a running commentary on the course *for your own benefit*. At its conclusion you will find that they have become a record of your own growth in consciousness.

1. Explain the relationship of man's mind to the Infinite Mind.
2. What is the great meaning of this to man?
3. What gave Jesus his attitude of authority?
4. How can we cultivate a sense of authority?
5. What is the difference between "technique" and "consciousness" in treatment?

WRITING SUGGESTIONS

Write out some definite ways in which you are going to increase your sense of authority in treatment.

READING SUGGESTIONS

It is not imperative that the student read the books suggested for collateral reading, but we strongly recommend that he do so for deeper insight into the subjects treated.

The books suggested may be available in your public library. If not, they may be purchased from our Book Department. Please consult our *Book Catalogue*.

Frederick Bailes, "Mopers, Hopers, Gropers, and Dopers"
Your Mind Can Heal You, Ch. VIII

THOUGHT-TRAINING FOR THE WEEK

Turn your thoughts this week to increasing your consciousness that whatever is true of Infinite Mind is true also of you. Use the ideas on page 5 to direct your thought.

A DAILY THOUGHT

Let this thought be your daily thought during the week that you study this lesson:

As long as the fear of the condition outweighs the knowledge of the power, one cannot be healed; when the knowledge of the power outweighs the fear of the condition, one can be healed.

A DAILY SELF-TREATMENT
(To be spoken quietly and thoughtfully each morning and evening)

"I know that my word is the word of power, that I can cope with any experience, that I neither fear nor expect evil, that I now fill my horizons with the expectancy of the good, and that I will dwell in the sunlight of this Healing Presence forever.

"I definitely speak my word to set Infinite Law into action. It follows the perfect pattern in my body, my business, my personal relationships. I shall be a blessing to everyone I meet this day. I will live expectantly, knowing that my good awaits me at every point and at every minute this day. I declare this to be the truth for all whose hearts are tuned to right action this day."

SCIENCE OF MIND

Home-Study Extension Course

(copyright 1951)

by

DR. FREDERICK BAILES

LESSON VII

THE TECHNIQUE OF TREATMENT

Jesus was the most successful healer who ever walked the earth. In his discourses he laid out clearly the fundamental principles which underlie all successful treatment; yet there is no record that he ever outlined the technique of treatment. This has been left for a modern age to discover and set forth.

Different healers have different methods of treatment, but they all fall into two main divisions. The first we shall call the REALIZA- TION Method, the second, the ANALYTICAL Method. The first is, probably, the one most frequently used by Jesus, although there is evidence that at times he also used the Analytical Method.

Since from this point on we shall use the term "practitioner" fre- quently, it will be well to explain that by it we mean anyone who practices the Science of Mind.

THE PRACTITIONER WORKS WITH HIS OWN THOUGHT ONLY

At the outset it must become clear to the student that, whichever method he is using, he is not trying primarily to influence the thought of the patient. What he does will eventually affect the patient's thought, but the purpose of the treatment is to keep the practitioner's OWN thought free from the patient's erroneous belief, and to convince the practitioner himself of the truth about the patient, which is that he is a perfect manifestation of the Infinite, and that whatever is true of the Infinite is necessarily true of the patient. The entire treatment is an action WITHIN the mind of the practitioner BY himself, UPON himself, but for the purpose of correcting the patient's false belief.

The practitioner knows that poverty, illness, or other adverse conditions manifesting in the realm of the physical are only distorted THOUGHTS that have taken form. He deals with them primarily. If, for instance, he is treating the sick, he remembers that man thinks, not alone with his brain, but with every single cell of his body; therefore, the illness is one of thought, the manifestation one of form. Thus he knows that the healing must be a healing of the destructive thought, and that this will result in a healed body. The latter will be called the healing by some, but the practitioner knows that it is only the OUTER MANIFESTATION of the real inward healing.

The practitioner sees the body not as flesh and bones, hard and unyielding, but as Spiritual Substance, whose form can be changed as easily as one would alter the form of a rising column of smoke by a slight movement of the finger through it. This realization enables him to hold the conviction of the alterability of the physical. As soon as his conviction concerning the patient is clear, without doubt or mental reservation, THE HEALING HAS OCCURRED. The treatment, therefore, is an operation of MIND that begins and ends in the thought of the practitioner; its fruits will be shown in the patient.

IN TREATMENT TALK ABOUT THE PATIENT— NOT TO HIM

When one treats another, the words in either method of treatment are always spoken in the THIRD person, never in the second. Thus we do not say, "You are well." We say "John Smith is well." The former tends toward hypnosis or suggestion; the latter is a statement of the truth which we believe concerning John Smith, who has been entertaining a false belief about himself.

When we treat ourselves, we use the first personal pronoun, "I," "me," "my," "mine."

THE REALIZATION METHOD OF TREATMENT

The REALIZATION Method is the simpler of the two methods. As its name implies, it is that movement of Mind by which we come instantly and simultaneously to a realization of the following:

1. The nothingness of the condition to be treated
2. The unchanged perfection which lies beneath the apparent ugly surface condition
3. The omnipotence of the Power which is directed toward the patient
4. The undeviating obedience of the Law which responds to the thought of the practitioner.

In using the Realization Method to treat for another, the practitioner would say, EITHER AUDIBLY OR TO HIMSELF, something like the following:

John Smith is the offspring of the Infinite; therefore, he partakes of the Divine nature, structure, and quality. This distorted condition is only the shadowing forth of his disturbed and distorted views of life and of himself; these thoughts are merely his beliefs. I refuse to accept his false concept of himself, knowing that the thought of the Infinite is that of perfection, wholeness, and well-being. I announce this truth to myself until there is no longer anything in my thought which questions the truth of my statement about John Smith.

The One perfect Life of the Infinite flows through John Smith now. It has always flowed through him. It is whole and complete. Nothing in the universe has the power to upset it or to obstruct it, for it is the resistless movement of Omnipotence in and through him.

His apparent illness is real only in a secondary sense. Perfection and wholeness are primary Reality. I look straight through the apparent reality to that which IS primary. One constructive thought is more potent than ten thousand destructive thoughts; therefore, I speak my declaration of Truth concerning John Smith with the quiet confidence that NOW, AT THIS VERY MOMENT, his illness is no more real than the horrors of a nightmare, and that he is awakening to his true state in which the false pictures of his nightmare disappear.

John Smith is NOW whole, complete, lacking nothing, for he is expressing the Divine nature, through the unhindered working of the Infinite Healing Presence in him; therefore, it MUST be so, and it IS so! I now release my word to DEEPER mind, turning the entire responsibility for the manifestation over to it.

CONCLUSION

With this, the practitioner RELEASES the healing process to the INFINITE HEALING PRESENCE, synonymous with Universal Mind and DEEPER mind, which is the only agency in the universe that changes thoughts into things, the only agency which possesses all the knowledge of the way to produce perfect cells in place of the former imperfect cells. He releases it with perfect confidence to DEEPER mind, where willingness to obey and the ability to do are the characteristics of this healing mind operating through Law. The way to RELEASE will be found in Lesson VIII, page 7.

HOW OFTEN TO TREAT

It is best to give treatment two or three times a day, always making sure to release the treatment to Infinite Mind, for it is "the Father who doeth the work." If we find ourselves coming back too often to treat again, it is a sign that we have not properly and completely released it.

If we are sure that "He is able [and willing] to keep that which I have committed unto Him" (2nd Tim. 1:12) we shall make a complete release. The Infinite never forgets; we have other things to divert our attention, but we can rest assured that the Infinite still carries that which we have committed unto it, and is changing the form accordingly.

EVERY TREATMENT A UNIT

Let every treatment be as though it were the ONLY treatment

that we are going to give that person. When we give another at the end of the day, let it be as though we were starting again at the beginning. Never allow the idea of time to enter in; by this we mean, do not say or think, "This is serious, and therefore will probably take a long time to heal." Remember, we are dealing with limitless power which can heal instantly, and would always heal instantly except for the barrier of our "time" thought or some other obstruction in the human consciousness.

GIVE THANKS

The moment that improvement shows, give thanks. Say, "That's good, Infinite Mind; I know you're on the job." From then on we merely touch the treatment lightly with our thought, as the child touches the hoop he rolls down the street after he as given it the initial movement. When tempted to treat too often, just say, "Well, I'm glad the Infinite Mind is working for John Smith." This is what we mean by touching lightly.

THE ANALYTICAL OR REASONING METHOD

The Analytical Method is more extensive, but better suited to those of an analytical turn of mind. The writer of this course uses it more often, because he prefers to approach such things from a reasoning point of view, and to analyze and dissect the process of treatment. There is an added benefit in it, because it breaks the treatment into seven steps; thus, when the results are not satisfactory, it furnishes an opportunity to determine at which step the treatment was not effective.

In the Analytical, or Reasoning, Method the treatment is comparable to a golf swing, which appears to the uninitiated to be one continuous movement, but is really a great many steps perfectly coordinated. The golfer must set his feet at exact positions, grasp the club, and, without taking his eyes off the ball, bring the club back slowly, and on the down-swing gradually accelerate its rate; then, after he has hit the ball, still keep his eyes on the spot where the ball had been. There are many components of a correct golf swing; these are given as examples.

When he is "off his game," a golfer can ask the instructor to play a round with him and watch him. If his trouble is a body sway, the professional will say, "I see where your trouble is. You're not keeping your body in line; you sway just a little as you make your stroke." When the golfer corrects this one step, his shots become good again. Yet, without breaking down the swing into its component parts, the instructor would have found it difficult to know just what the golfer was doing that was not correct.

It is for the same purpose that we have broken down ANALYT-ICAL treatment into seven steps. We call these steps the Seven "R's."

THE SEVEN "R'S" OF THE ANALYTICAL METHOD
FIRST "R"—RELAXATION
1. PHYSICAL RELAXATION

There must be both bodily and mental relaxation. Assume a position in which there is as little physical tension as possible. The posture doesn't matter so much — some treat standing, some sitting, some walking quietly, some lying down—but one must be physically relaxed.

Regarding position: When one falls asleep, as happens when the SURFACE mind goes off the job, he tends to assume a recumbent position. This proves that one consciously has to use direction over the muscles to maintain a standing or sitting position, but we can do this so easily that we don't notice we are maintaining a certain muscular tension in any but the lying down position; therefore, the least tensed (or most relaxed) position is that of lying down. This means that all our thought, both SURFACE and DEEPER, can go into the treatment.

Yet, unconsciously, sometimes the fingers will clench, or in some way the muscles of the body will tense; so it is always well to "shake oneself out" all over to be sure one has achieved complete relaxation.

2. MENTAL AND EMOTIONAL RELAXATION

More important, however, is mental and emotional relaxation. A tensed practitioner simply cannot get results, no matter how well he has learned the techniques of treatment. The student must remember that ALL of himself goes into his treatment. This means that no matter what WORDS he uses to formulate the truth, a tenseness in his inner self will completely nullify those words.

Words are secondary to the myriad streams of deeper thought which sweep in and swirl about a treatment. Since a person is the sum total of all he has ever experienced, if there are deeply hidden and, as yet, unresolved conflicts within him, these will affect his treatment to the degree of their intensity, because ALL mental and emotional undercurrents enter into a treatment.

IMPERFECT PERSONS CAN TREAT SUCCESSFULLY

This does not mean that the practitioner must be near-perfect in order to heal. It does mean that if he carries a crippling memory of some past hurt, he must do something about it. Any experience that leads to self-pity must be healed. Any person who thinks that life has not treated him fairly, or who carries a grudge against someone who has wronged him, positively MUST resolve that problem if he is to be a good practitioner.

Jesus hinted at this when he said, "Therefore, if thou bring thy gift to the altar, and there rememberest that thy brother hath ought against thee; leave there thy gift before the altar and go thy way; first be reconciled to thy brother, and then come and offer thy gift." (Matt. 5:23-24)

At first sight this might look as though it referred to getting straight with someone that we have wronged. But it applies equally to OUR feeling of being wronged. The net result of either experience is a feeling of separation. The practitioner must have a feeling of oneness with all. He can hold no hard feelings. It may not be possible, or even necessary, that he go in person to have matters straightened out. The chief necessity is that he straighten out HIS OWN feelings toward those who have wronged or hurt him.

CLEANSE THE INNER LIFE

Envy is another tensing emotion. The practitioner must be clean from all feelings of envy toward anyone more successful, more prosperous, more attractive, or healthier. It is quite understandable that we wish we were blessed as some others are blessed, and this is well;

but the positive attitude toward this wishing should be a quiet determination to emulate their success. The attainment of others can be turned into the spark that fires us to greater endeavor; thus it becomes a constructive stimulus.

Envy is negative, because it spells separation from others. By seeing their success as something distant from us, we unconsciously feel separated from them. Unless we rejoice with them, we are really believing that the greater heights attained by somone else are denied to us. On the other hand, the desire to emulate is positive, because it spells unification. It is the viewing of greater heights with which we may unify ourselves in consciousness, see ourselves experiencing them, and thereby set in motion the law that will bring us to them. The very feeling that we are on our way, even though we have not yet arrived, is conducive to relaxation, because it is free from any bitterness at our less satisfactory performance.

Jealousy, censoriousness, and any other hostile feelings must vanish also, for they are definitely separative feelings.

THE WHOLE LIFE GOES INTO THE TREATMENT

It can readily be seen that to be a successful practitioner, one must maintain a high standard of life. This, really, is the only satisfying kind of life, for it is the pathway to peace and to achievement of the goals every one of us desires to reach, whether we wish to study further and become professional practitioners or not. It means building into the character those elements of serenity, courage, optimism, and good will which make for an attractive personality, and which also lay the foundation for excellent health and prosperity.

While this sort of character makes for success in any profession, it is imperative in a practitioner. He who is sunk in gloom cannot treat others into a state of happiness. He who is burdened with debt does not easily treat others into prosperity. He who would save others from adverse circumstances must first save himself.

Yet, he need not be. completely free before he starts treating. Remembering that the outer manifestation is only the shadow of that which first was formed on the hidden side of his life, he achieves a CONSCIOUSNESS of his freedom before his outward circumstances manifest it. The reality is the thought. If he has faced his difficulties and has achieved a reasonable mastery over them, he can begin to treat others. But, we repeat, the first step in successful treating is a RELAXED MIND.

SECOND "R"—RECOGNITION

The second step is RECOGNITION. We must recognize that we are surrounded by an ocean of Mind, in which lie the answers to all the problems of the world, a Mind which is characterized by Omnipotence, Omniscience, and Omnipresence, and WHICH IS COMPLETELY OBEDIENT, OR RESPONSIVE, TO OUR THOUGHT.

1. OMNIPOTENCE—ALL POWER

With regard to Omnipotence, we recognize that we are dealing with ALL the power in the universe. Thinking of God quantitatively, the average human thinks that if a certain amount of power is exercised at a certain point, there must be less left for other points. In the SCIENCE OF MIND we endeavor to see that at all times ALL of God is present at any point where ANY of God is, and that no matter at how many points the healing streams are flowing, there is just as much flowing through our word for this person whom we are treating as there was before, and just as much for our own needs as we can take.

In this sense, all men are "the only-begotten of the Father." One of the concepts that gave Jesus his tremendous sense of authority over conditions was that he considered himself "the only-begotten Son." (John 3:16)

To illustrate: Suppose that John Smith is the richest man in the world. His son, James Smith, is his only heir. Everything the father has is for the son alone as though there were not another person in the world. James Smith lives in a very vivid sense of security. If he has a need, he merely has to write a check, or mention it to his father, and that need is fulfilled. To someone who remonstrates, the father might say, "What's the difference? It will all be his some day. For that matter, it is his now; so if he needs anything, there's no reason why he should not draw upon what is potentially his."

Jesus saw the true inner meaning of Omnipotence. He saw that each person in the world could consider himself the heir to all the power there is, for there is no such thing as a division here. All of Omnipotence is present where any of it is. Each man can consider himself the recipient of EVERYTHING the Father has or is, without depriving anyone else. In this sense all men are the only-begotten, and they become "full of grace and truth" (John 1:14) as they come to understand this.

Thus, when we treat, we call in, not a platoon of soldiers, but the entire army, and our neighbor does the same with the entire army at the same time. This is the recognition which makes a powerful practitioner.

2. OMNISCIENCE—ALL KNOWLEDGE

We now consider the second phase—Omniscience. There is not a problem in the universe to which Omniscience does not know the answer. Omniscience has brought into being everything that is. It has built every cell of the body, every successful life, for "without it was not anything made that was made." (John 1:3) Man has problems; Omniscience has nothing but answers; it knows nothing of problems. Its knowledge is so far beyond ANYTHING that man has yet discovered that it knows nothing of "incurable" diseases. Man is proud of his scientific "discoveries"; yet Omniscience knew them all before the foundation of the world.

3. OMNIPRESENCE—EVERYWHERE PRESENT

The third phase, Omnipresence, means that the Infinite is equally present at all points in space; therefore, one can treat a person living on the other side of the world just as easily as if he were in the same room. The practitioner does not squirt his thought at the person he is treating; if he did, the treatment would become weaker in direct ratio to the distance.

During a treatment the practitioner substitutes his perfect thought about the patient for the patient's imperfect thought about himself. He releases his perfect thought into that Infinite Mind which is present everywhere, and this Mind proceeds to fabricate that perfect thought into form. The Infinite Mind, streaming also through the patient, now carries his picture of perfect health, which becomes the state of the patient.

The next lesson will bring this out even more clearly. We have covered only the first two steps in treatment in this lesson.

SPECIAL HELPS IN STUDYING THE LESSON

These study-helps have been carefully prepared to help you get the most out of this course.

QUESTIONS

Educators have found that a series of questions enables the student to get a complete picture of the material studied. You will find the questions accompanying each lesson highly valuable in uncovering concepts which you might otherwise pass by.

We advise that you first study the lesson carefully, then put it aside, write the answers to the question, and, finally, *check your answers by the lesson.*

Keep the answers as a running commentary on the course *for your own benefit.* At its conclusion you will find that they have become a record of your own growth in consciousness.

1. What is the purpose of treatment?
2. Why do we use the third person instead of the second in treatment?
3. Explain the Realization Method.
4. Why is it so important that we release a treatment?
5. What is the tremendous significance of Omnipotence, Omniscience, and Omnipresence?

WRITING SUGGESTION

Write a treatment for yourself or for another following the Realization Method.

READING SUGGESTIONS

It is not imperative that the student read the books suggested for collateral reading, but we strongly recommend that he do so for deeper insight into the subjects treated.

The books suggested may be available in your public library. If not, they may be purchased from our Book Department. Please consult our *Book Catalogue*.

Frederick Bailes, *Your Mind Can Heal You,*
          Ch. V (pp. 99-106), Ch. X (227-29)
David Seabury, *How Jesus Heals Our Minds Today*, 297-317
Margery Wilson, *Your Personality and God*, Ch. III

THOUGHT-TRAINING FOR THE WEEK

Examine your thought and if you find anything that is keeping you from a relaxed mind, say to yourself, "I bring this out into the open, take a final look at it, and then know that it is blotted out forever by the Peace of the One Mind."

A DAILY THOUGHT

Let this thought be your daily thought during the week that you study this lesson:

We are surrounded by an ocean of Mind—all-powerful, all-knowing, everywhere present — in which we live, move, and have our being.

A DAILY SELF-TREATMENT

(To be spoken quietly and thoughtfully each morning and evening)
"This day I enter into a conscious acceptance of harmony. I let go of all hurt feelings, even though I may have felt that they have a legitimate basis. I freely forgive myself for allowing myself to be hurt, and I generously forgive those whose words or actions gave rise to my inharmony.

"I affirm this day that the entire hidden universe backs me in my endeavors, that hidden currents of energy from the Divine Mind are now my inspiration, that everything in the universe is united in a benevolent conspiracy for my good. I give of my love and my kindness this day, and I confidently expect the same from everyone I meet."

SCIENCE OF MIND

Home-Study Extension Course

(copyright 1951)

by

DR. FREDERICK BAILES

LESSON VIII

THE TECHNIQUE OF TREATMENT
(continued)

THIRD "R"—RELATIONSHIP

The third "R" in treatment is RELATIONSHIP. Having brought oneself into the properly relaxed state, physically and mentally, and having come into a recognition of the Power with which he works, the practitioner might still feel that he is not a part of this Power. He might agree that It exists as part of the nature of the Infinite, but that he himself, being a struggling, faulty human being, is something apart and separate from It. It is important, therefore, that he comes into a clear understanding of his relationship to this Power. To acquire this understanding, it is necessary to go into the varied interpretations of the nature of God.

THE NATURE OF THE INFINITE

Throughout the ages, theologians have manfully struggled with this concept. They have done their best, but their efforts range all the way from the crude concepts of primitive man, through the stiff dogmas of the Dark and Middle Ages, to the more enlightened concepts of modern man. Yet, in this Twentieth Century all three of these types of thinking prevail in various religious circles, and, unfortunately, some men who secretly think differently are compelled to preach archaic gospels or lose their pulpits and their livelihood.

Probably the key to the question lies in one's view of the Personality of God. IS GOD PERSONALITY OR IMPERSONAL PRINCIPLE? We believe that He is a combination of both.

ETERNALITY OF ENERGY AND SUBSTANCE

Lesson IV showed the three phases of the Trinity to be Spirit, Mind, and Body. Neither one created the others, for all three were from the beginning, the only exception being that Body was not yet formed; It was present then only as the Primary Unformed Substance of the universe.

The principles of the conservation of matter and the conservation of energy state, in effect, that matter and energy are equally indestructible and, therefore, are eternal in that their sum total is never increased nor diminished, but merely changed from one form into another. A piece of paper burns up, yet does not go out of existence except in its papery form. It has changed its form into ash and gases; yet none of it has been rendered nonexistent. There is always the same amount.

A meteorite passing through the earth's atmosphere has motion, which is converted into heat; then the heat is converted into light; but the quantity is never diminished.

The term "God" is difficult to define, for everything seen and unseen is some part of this Trinity that we call God. Our bodies are the extension of the unformed Substance, which is the Body of God. Our minds are the extension of the God-Mind. Our spirit is the extension of God as Spirit. Man is linked at every point to the God-Trinity. Man expresses very imperfectly in the relative that which God is in the Perfect Absolute.

GOD AS IMPERSONAL PRINCIPLE

Our RELATIONSHIP, therefore, is both personal and impersonal. The atmosphere, which is part of the body of God, presses impersonally and equally upon each of the two billions of earth's inhabitants.

Life, that greatest of all mysteries, flows impersonally through us all. Contrary to the opinion of many, material supply flows impersonally throughout the universe, and is drawn toward the person whose consciousness attracts it. The universe is impersonal toward its inhabitants in that the sun and rain fall upon all; the earth will respond to anyone's cultivation, the seas will float anyone's boat; gravitation pulls all men equally.

In like manner, the stream of consciousness will quite impersonally make one person well and another ill, according to the quality of their thought. Thought flows by law just as electricity does, and will destroy one or build one up, just as electricity will make toast for us or electrocute us, DEPENDING UPON WHETHER WE ADJUST TO OR VIOLATE THE LAW OF ITS ACTION.

From this point of view, there is a phase of God which is entirely impersonal, operating equally everywhere in this impersonal manner. When man understands this, he no longer will rail against God for the damage done by cyclone, earthquake, and tornado, which are the result of natural law, and which have an ultimate stabilizing effect in the structure and operation of the physical universe. A reasoning man adjusts to meteorological violence either by not settling in that district, or by making provision for it. God does not force him to live there any more than He forces him to build his house on a sand dune.

In like manner, the metaphysically instructed man will no longer shriek against God over the death of his loved one, even if it is a little child, for he will understand that it is his ignorance of, or ill-adjustment to, mental law that has set in motion those destructive forces called disease.

To answer an unspoken question at this point, we might interject that the bodies of infants and small children usually reflect the buried thought-patterns of the parents, nurses, or relatives, more than their own; and these older persons, as well as the child, should be treated for the child's illness.

THE PERSONAL QUALITY OF GOD

So much for the impersonal side of the nature of God as evidenced in the vast field of what we call mental and physical law. But man introduces the personal element when he begins to recognize or to seek union with the Infinite.

Rufus Jones has used an appropriate term—the "Double Search." He reasons that man has an instinct for God which impels him ever to seek to find his way back into union with the Infinite. But he says that man's search is only the answering search; the Original Search is that of the Infinite for union with man.

Man's predecessors came from that long line of physical organisms dating back to the first living cell. Each of those predecessors was of a lower order than man; therefore, they were incapable of originating a spiritual impulse; so his spiritual outreaching could not have come from his physical nature. This spiritual hunger, then, must be the outreaching of God for man, and man's desire for union with the Infinite must be his intuitive response to this, hence the term "Double Search."

We mentioned before the difficulty of defining God or describing His nature with any detailed accuracy, but it is at the point of man's intuitive response to the Original Search that God becomes personal. There must be some larger sense in which God is personal, but it is far beyond the comprehension of finite man who invariably connects personality with form or with the attributes which we associate with our human personality. The way the Law of Creativeness responds to man's thought makes it seem humanly personal, so that it is, at the same time, both personal and impersonal. More than this it is not necessary to say at this time.

RELATIONSHIP OF KIND RATHER THAN OF DEGREE

The relationship, then, is that of a union of KIND rather than of DEGREE. That which is in harmony tends to unify with this which is in the same harmony. It follows, then, that as our thought clears itself of earthiness, it moves into closer harmony with that of the Infinite, and a close working bond is established.

For example, he whose heart is filled with hate and prejudice cannot establish the right relationship with Creative Law, which springs from a Love Source. He who is filled with fear is not in unison with that which has never known fear.

We do not have to be perfect in our mental freedom, but we must be willing and ready to drop the ugly, deforming thought-patterns if we are to move into this relationship which precedes the healing of ourselves and others.

LIKE UNITES WITH LIKE

So long as we are willing to let go those destructive moods, we are establishing the proper relationship with the Infinite. Thus we are to that extent merged with His thought, which can then flow through our thought-patterns with all its healing knowledge, for, in the final analysis, it is always the Infinite Healing Presence that heals.

It has been said, "In Him we live and move and have our being." (Acts 17:28). This is the original part of the Double Search; but the responsive part is that in which WE let HIM "live, move, and have His being" in us. We in Him, He in us.

It is as though we should toss a biscuit into the ocean. It would be IN THE OCEAN, but, as it stayed there, the ocean would gradually seep through it and be in it.

The good practitioner—and remember that by "practitioner" we mean anyone who practices the SCIENCE OF MIND—is a God-saturated person, forever drawing upon all the abilities of that which saturates him, and forever yielding to that which saturates. His power lies NOT in himself, but in that with which he is in relationship. He whose relationship is closer with the negative will manifest the negative. He whose closer harmonies are with that which is "true, honest, just, pure, lovely, and of good report" (Phil. 4:8) will manifest these.

FOURTH "R"—REASONING

The fourth "R" is REASONING. In the Analytical Method of treatment, this is used more than in the Realization Method; yet even in the latter there is a lightning-like or instantaneous reasoning.

WHY WE REASON

Reasoning is for the purpose of dissolving the practitioner's doubts.

We must remember that the treatment begins and ends within the mind of the practitioner, in that he works upon HIS OWN belief rather than on that of the patient; thus we shall see the value of reasoning.

Let us suppose a man comes to us to be healed of a disease. We start to treat by immediately declaring his perfection, but at once an image of his disability comes before us. Perhaps the doctor has told him that his condition is incurable, and this prognosis comes before us. The memory of our own faults or any one of a hundred different forms of negative thinking rises to make us waver. To dispel these doubts and ugly pictures we resort to reasoning.

HOW WE REASON

We begin by calling up memories of someone else who had this or another equally "incurable" condition, and we argue with ourselves that the Infinite Healing Presence was well able to deal with it, because the sufferer was completely healed. At first we shall need to think of healings we have heard of or read about, but soon we ourselves shall have treated persons back into health. Then we can call upon our own experience.

Again, we may begin to reason about the undefeatable power of the Omnipotent Infinite as shown in and through nature. We think of the tremendous force which holds a myriad suns in place, moving them effortlessly through space, always on time to the spilt second. Then we argue with ourselves that this apparently big problem which confronts us is infinitesimal to such a Power.

Thus we reason our way to the point where all our inner objections are answered, and all inner doubts are removed. We reason that the condition is entirely a thing of thought, and that constructive thought is ten thousand times more powerful than destructive thought; therefore, this constructive thought of ours, being brought into line with the Infinite, is in line with the Infinite Will, and has power over the destructive pattern.

We remember that we treat the THOUGHT rather than the physical condition, and that, as the thought alters, there will be a corresponding change in the physical.

FIFTH "R"—REALIZATION
CERTAINTY THAT OUR WORD REGISTERS

The fifth "R" is REALIZATION.. At this stage, we realize that we are not speaking our word into a void, but that we are impressing it upon the receptive mind of the Infinite. We realize that there is not the slightest reason that our word should not have power and not the least occasion for doubt and, furthermore, not any reluctance upon the part of the Infinite to flow into form in accordance with this perfect picture we are presenting to it. And we are so convinced of the truth of our conviction that any failure would be impossible.

KNOWING IS HIGHER THAN FEELING

In this stage, there may be a sense of great uplift, or there may be none. Remember, our feelings lie in the field of emotions, which might or might not back up our conviction; therefore, do not feel that the treatment has not been a good one if the rising tide of emotion is absent. It is well when we FEEL the truth we are declaring, but it is infinitely better when we KNOW the truth we are declaring. Knowing is always higher than feeling, and our demonstrations are made upon that which we know, rather than upon that which we feel.

On the other hand, times will come when the practitioner is lifted to a very lofty altitude, when it seems as if the earth recedes and the spiritual world becomes very real. Doubts, uncertainties, and self-condemnation are all passed away, and one enters into a sense of union with. the Infinite which is so real that he feels there never were any problems, and never will be any. Don't seek this, but if it comes, surrender yourself to it, for it is a high point of realization.

SIXTH "R"—RELEASE

The sixth "R" is RELEASE. When one comes to the place where his doubts have been replaced by a deep conviction, he quickly moves on to the next stage, which is RELEASE. Keeping in mind that it is not WE who produce the results, we quickly release our perfectly formed picture of our patient to the Infinite Mind, which is always entirely receptive to our thought.

This Creative Mind is the only agency in the universe that can transform thoughts into things; in fact, this is what It is doing every moment of time. It has turned our patient's destructive thought into illness. It will now turn our constructive thought into health as it flows through him.

We shall conceive this Infinite Mind to be like a river, into which the thoughts of the race are constantly falling. Its business is constantly to fabricate these thoughts into form. This river flows equally through all men, and is called their minds as It passes through their brains. Healing others at a distance is possible, because Infinite Mind receives our perfect thought and carries it through that one whom we are treating. (In fact, It carries it through all men, but not all are responsive.)

Thus it is not a question of how much mental force the practitioner can generate to force his mental pattern over a great distance to someone else; the secret of healing lies in the completeness with which one releases his thought and word to this River of Mind.

RESPONSIBILITY IS ON MIND, NOT ON US

Having released it, we drop all responsibility for making our word come to pass. That responsibility belongs to Mind. Ours is only to make sure that we release as perfect a picture to that Mind as is possible. We don't try to push it or help in any way except by not allowing discordant or doubtful thoughts to enter our mind in regard to the one treated. "The FATHER that dwelleth in me, He doeth the works." (John 14:10). "I know whom I have believed and am persuaded that HE is able to keep that which I have committed unto HIM against that day [of manifestation]." (II Tim. 1:12)

To repeat what was said in an earlier lesson, it is sufficient to treat two or three times daily for the person. If you find yourself trying to treat too often, it is a sign that you have not released the treatment completely. Whenever the thought of the patient enters your mind during the day, just say, "I'm glad I've turned it over to the Infinite Mind," and release it again.

Releasing is the most important part of treatment. Unfortunately, some beginners, as well as some experienced students, have difficulty in learning to release completely. Try to step out from under the sense of responsibility. Let your thought about the person himself go completely into the care of the Infinite. We should not think steadily all day of each person that we treat, but rather should turn our treatment over to the Infinite, which easily carries our thought about all our patients. It never forgets. It never grows weary. Release! Release! Release!

SEVENTH "R"—REJOICING

The seventh "R" is REJOICING. One never is happy over things which do not come to pass. He rejoices at completion and accomplishment; therefore, we give thanks as soon as we have released our word to the Infinite. This is "giving substance to things hoped for, giving evidence to things not seen." (Heb. 11:1)

Rejoicing and giving thanks are not done for the purpose of influencing the Infinite. They are done for their effect upon the practitioner. If an unreliable person promises to give us something at a later date, and especially if his promises were never kept in the past, we might politely thank him; but inwardly there would be no rejoicing, because we would not believe he would fulfill his promise.

But if a loved one who always keeps his word promises us something in the future, we immediately begin to rejoice in it, even before we have it in our hands, because we actually believe, in fact we KNOW, that he will give it. Our belief in the Infinite responsiveness leads us to give thanks at once, and our giving thanks helps confirm our confidence in It.

These are the seven component parts of the treatment. Now for the actual treatment.

WHAT A TREATMENT IS

A treatment consists of the formulation of a concept of perfection, accompanied by a conviction of its truth with the assurance that the Creative Law of Mind, through Omniscience, Omnipotence, and Omnipresence, invariably proceeds to translate it into form.

In simpler language, a treatment is the releasing of our highest thought about a person or a condition with the assurance that Infinite

Creative Mind begins immediately to bring to pass that which we have embodied in the treatment.

PRACTICAL POINTS IN TREATMENT

1. WE USE THE THIRD PERSON

As we said in the preceding lesson, a treatment for another is always carried on in the third person, never in the second; that is, we never say, "John Smith, YOU are well," instead we say, "John Smith is well." We talk ABOUT the patient, not TO him. That which we say TO him in an interview is not a treatment. That which we say ABOUT him when he is not with us is the treatment.

2. WE DO NOT PETITION

We offer no petition in the treatment. We do not say, "Please grant healing to him." Instead, we make declarations and assertions ABOUT him, his perfect thought, and his freedom from false beliefs, and end the treatment by saying that his body and his whole outer affairs are now manifesting his changed belief.

3. WE SPEAK WITH AUTHORITY

We go further. "Thou shalt DECREE a thing, and it shall be established unto thee." (Job 22:28). We inject a note of authority into our treatment so that instead of begging or hoping that something will happen, we DECREE that it shall happen. This does not mean that we are "bossing" God. It means that we recognize the Creative Law as being completely obedient to our spoken word. We do not "boss" the grocery clerk, but we do order a pound of butter, and we fully expect him to hand it to us. We would be amazed if he should tell us he doesn't think butter is good for us; therefore, he must refuse to give it to us. We decree butter for us; he obeys our decree.

CULTIVATE EXPECTANCY OF RESULTS

In the beginning, some students are astounded when the Law works for them. They should be astounded when It seems not to work for them. Naturally, there is rejoicing when we see our spoken word coming into form, but soon this is replaced by a more settled expectancy as we see more and more manifestations coming forth in response to our treatment.

"Each victory will help you some other to win." Don't wait until you are perfect.

SPECIAL HELPS IN STUDYING THE LESSON

These study-helps have been carefully prepared to help you get the most out of this course.

QUESTIONS

Educators have found that a series of questions enables the student to get a complete picture of the material studied. You will find the questions accompanying each lesson highly valuable in uncovering concepts which you might otherwise pass by.

We advise that you first study the lesson carefully, then put it aside, write the answers to the questions, and, finally, *check your answers by the lesson.*

Keep the answers as a running commentary on the course *for your own benefit.* At its conclusion you will find that they have become a record of your own growth in consciousness.

1. Why do we say that man's relationship to God is of kind rather than of degree?
2. Why is the Realization Step the high point of treatment?
3. Why is the Release Step so important?
4. What is the purpose of the Rejoicing Step?
5. Why do we talk *about* rather than *to* the person in a treatment?

WRITING SUGGESTION

Write a treatment for yourself or another following the Analytical, or Reasoning, Method, and giving careful attention to the Seven "R's."

READING SUGGESTIONS

It is not imperative that the student read the books suggested for collateral reading, but we strongly recommend that he do so for deeper insight into the subjects treated.

The books suggested may be available in your public library. If not, they may be purchased from our Book Department. Please consult our *Book Catalogue*.

Edith Armstrong, "Help Yourself"
Frederick Bailes, *Your Mind Can Heal You*, Ch. V (pp. 106-18)
Bessie Beihl, *The Lord Is Your Shepherd*

THOUGHT-TRAINING FOR THE WEEK

In order to bring yourself into a closer relationship with the Infinite, test your thought this week by Phil. 4:8. Is it true, honest, just, pure, lovely, and of good report?

A DAILY THOUGHT

Let this thought be your daily thought during the week that you study this lesson:

Man has a homing instinct which impels him ever to seek for a way back into union with the Infinite.

A DAILY SELF-TREATMENT
(To be spoken quietly and thoughtfully each morning and evening)

"This day I seek the consciousness of the Divine Presence, so near and warm that it seems closer than breathing, and nearer than hands or feet. It is a steadying influence which says, 'Lo, I am with you alway.'

"The Divine Companion is mine. I draw inwardly upon the unseen currents of power which flood my entire being. Infinite Wisdom is my inner teacher, and becomes a lamp unto my feet and a light unto my path. The Infinite Healing Presence steals silently throughout my entire body and through all my affairs."

SCIENCE OF MIND
Home-Study Extension Course

(copyright 1951)

by

DR. FREDERICK BAILES

LESSON IX

TREATMENT FOR SPECIFIC CONDITIONS

The remainder of this introductory course will be devoted to the ways of treating various kinds of difficulties if and when they appear.

The student must never forget that we treat the THOUGHT, rather than the condition. This is because the condition is only the thought in form. Conditions are only effects; thoughts are the causes. Correct the causes and the effects correct themselves. We resolve the condition back into thought; then we dissolve the thought through treatment.

HOW TO TREAT STOMACH ULCERS

Suppose we start with a physical condition such as stomach ulcers. There is nothing more physical in its manifestation than this ailment, and nothing more mental in its cause. One can persistently treat for the ULCERS themselves to heal, and see no result. But when one treats for the underlying IRRITATION, the ulcers heal.

THE CAUSE IS A FALSE BELIEF OF IRRITATION

Ulcers come in that person who has the false belief that something or someone outside of himself has the power to irritate him. The source of his irritation might be members of his family, those with or for whom he works, an environment with which he is not in agreement, the pressure of overwork, financial worries, or any one of a number of external experiences.

We have said that while man thinks with every cell of his body, the cell has no individual intelligence, no pattern of thought OTHER THAN THAT OF THE PERSON of whom it is a part. The waves of thought from the brain, carried over the network of fine threads called the nervous system, are momentarily sweeping the entire body; therefore, the cell has to think that which the brain thinks, and the brain has to think that which the person using the brain thinks.

NOTHING CAN IRRITATE US
WITHOUT OUR CONSENT

Things or experiences in themselves have no power to irritate us. It is OUR REACTIONS to them which irritate. One person may say, "Green and red irritate and enrage me." The other says, "I simply adore red and green." Another says, "That Mrs. Smith's shrill cackle drives me wild." Her neighbor says, "I love to hear Mrs. Smith's merry laugh." Now, if there were some irritating quality IN the colors or the laugh, it would irritate all equally, as does acid when spilled on the back of the hand; therefore, the irritation arises WITHIN the person and is HIS irritated reaction to something that is neutral.

The person who understands the SCIENCE OF MIND knows that nothing in the universe has the inherent power to irritate him WITHOUT HIS CONSENT. He, therefore, withholds his consent. He chooses to hold quiet and steady in the presence of that which others allow to irritate them, and he thus remains free from irritation.

He who does not understand this is allowing himself to be irritated hourly. Those successive waves of thought flashing throughout the body begin to impart their irritating nature to the cells through which they pass. Certain organs and tissues seem to be more susceptible to irritation than others; therefore, he finds an irritation of the skin or perhaps of a mucous membrane, starting to bother him. Sinus trouble which has not been affected by change of climate has often been healed by healing the belief in irritation, as have all the various body conditions which arise from this false belief. HEAL THE THOUGHT, AND THE BODY WILL HEAL ITSELF.

SAMPLE TREATMENT FOR IRRITATION

A treatment for this condition might be carried along the following lines. The student may alter or add to it to suit his own consciousness and the conditions involved:

I know that John Smith is an extension of Infinite Mind; therefore, what is true of It must be true of him.

Nothing in the universe has the power to irritate or disturb the Infinite, for It rests always in a state of perfect peace.

John Smith's false belief in the cause of his irritation has produced a bodily irritation. I now speak my perfect word, declaring that nothing in the universe has the power to irritate him, and that he knows this truth to be operating around and within him at this moment.

This new belief makes him quiet and serene in the presence of the most disturbing situations. He is held steady and tranquil by the action of Spirit deep within him. Peace is an ever-present reality to him.

New brain waves are sweeping over his body. The cells love this new-found peace; they rapidly build themselves according to the perfect pattern. The Infinite Healing presence fills each cell with so much of Itself that there is no room for anything else.

I release this word about John Smith of 1111 Manchester Road, giving thanks for its perfect manifestation, before I see it in form. My word decrees it into form; therefore it MUST BE SO, and IT IS SO.

NAME THE PERSON

A treatment is a very definite thing, for a definite purpose, in a definite person; therefore, we give the name and address of the person treated. If for some reason we do not know the address, the name will be specific enough for our purpose.

TREATING THE BELIEF

It will be noticed that the only reference to the body is near the conclusion of the treatment. We lightly touch it in passing to indicate the specific condition treated, but we do not overstress it. Sometimes we use the words, "And I know that every cell of his body knows this truth which I speak, and is being remolded according to it."

It is important that we see clearly that man IS an extension of the Infinite, as the inlet is of the ocean. This is to establish a basis of oneness upon which we can base our expectation of healing.

In one sense there is nothing to heal. The illness lies in the false belief. The inner world is the world of Reality; the outer world is that of the shadow thrown by the inner. There is no doubt but that a pain is real to our senses, or that a broken bone is broken, but the Infinite never experiences pain or fracture; therefore, our healing comes to the degree that we can establish our sense of ONENESS OF QUALITY with the Infinite, remembering that the Infinite is Reality, the body is shadow.

BURIED RACIAL BELIEFS—THE RACE MIND

If man had advanced to the stage where there was a universal DISbelief in pain and break, there would be neither of these for him to experience. Neither would there be any of the miserable conditions under which mankind labors. But we have not yet reached that stage, and so we in the SCIENCE OF MIND have to use whatever method we, as individuals, can use to separate ourselves from the false racial beliefs, and establish a personal belief of the unreality, or impermanence, of ANY experience which limits man's freedom. This personal belief is, at present, widely at variance with commonly accepted beliefs; therefore, it is not always easy to free ourselves from the drag of the race-thought.

This should not discourage us, nor should we be disheartened because the race is only starting its climb into spiritual realms; on the contrary, we should be very happy because it has made so much progress in so short a time. One encouraging feature is that the moment our personal belief can be lifted even a little higher, our outer manifestation will automatically rise that much higher. Even if we cannot rise into perfection immediately, we can at least grow in that direction, and there will be enough encouraging demonstrations to keep us moving upward.

RECOGNIZE THAT YOU ARE THE INFINITE BOUNDED BY FORM

We repeat that a drop of sea water differs from the ocean only in size. Each drop chemically analyzes as does the ocean. As far as water is concerned, the inlet IS the ocean, the only difference being that it is "boundarized" into smaller form by shores that are easily seen. *Man,* as we have said in a previous lesson, *is the Infinite bounded by form.* This we must remember as we treat ourselves and others, for it is the key to mental and spiritual healing.

SPEAK WITH AUTHORITY

A treatment differs from the ordinary concept of prayer in that we do not abase ourselves, calling ourselves sinners and worms of the dust. We stand upon our inherent dignity as extensions of the Infinite. We speak with authority because we know that we reproduce the Creative Cycle that brought the world into being, and that, because of our unique relationship to God, our word could be as powerful as that of God if we could shake ourselves free of the race-thought and actually believe, with all our hearts, that this IS SO.

CONFIDENTLY SPEAK YOUR WORD

We do not merely wish or hope for something to happen. We speak our word, KNOWING that it will happen. In treatment there is a decisiveness that is lacking in the older-style prayers, which frequently wobbled, because the person praying was never sure that what he was asking for was according to the will of God.

We have seen, during the course of these lessons, that the will of God is anything that enlarges us or our happiness without hurting someone else. It is our duty to determine the integrity of our prayer (treatment) from this point of view. Then, having done this, we can treat with the completest assurance that there is nothing in the universe that wishes us not to have what we ask for.

FALSE BELIEF OF STRINGENCY

Suppose the condition to be treated is one of supply. We do not treat that money will pour into the life of this person, even though that is what he wants, and we want him to have it. In the Sermon on the Mount (Matt. 5-7) Jesus was dealing with deep underlying beliefs. In the sixth chapter he came to the subject of supply. He admitted that the people's desire for food and clothing was legitimate, but he tried to show them that if they would seek the Giver, the gifts would naturally follow.

He talked of spiritually conceived supply while their minds were on money. He talked of an inner life hidden within the lilies of the field, which clothed the flowers with an outer beauty; but they were thinking of garments to cover their bodies. He talked of an endless store of supply which had always been present there to keep the sparrows alive, but they were thinking of loaves of bread. In effect he said: "For the time being, forget those things of sense and seek the inner kingdom of God; unite your consciousness with that of the Giver, who has never known lack; then, as a matter of course, these secondary things will all be added to you."

SPIRITUAL BASIS FOR SUPPLY

The man who sees loaves of bread and overcoats ONLY, or sees them as the chief end of life, will have to scratch daily for another loaf and another coat. But he who drives past the loaf to the underlying PRINCIPLE of an unfailing supply will quietly KNOW that there will be another loaf tomorrow. Though this distinction might not seem significant, IT IS ONE OF THE MOST IMPORTANT WE CAN MAKE, for the following reasons:

The Healing Principle is far wider than health, which is only one of its manifestations. The Principle of Supply is far more extensive than money or food, which are only two of its manifestations. The Principle of Harmony is universal, rather than just individual peace of mind; the latter is merely one of its manifestations. Underlying all THINGS we must find the principle of that thing; then we can apply that principle to a thousand particulars.

The Kingdom of God, so often mentioned by Jesus, is the CONSCIOUSNESS OF THE ONENESS OF GOD AND MAN.

This Kingdom is sought by breaking free from the mass view, constantly lifting our thought to its highest levels, and seeing God as never reluctant to grant our desires, but rather ever seeking to express a more abundant life through us. It is the putting away of that which is petty, cruel, and censorious toward others, seeing them as also seeking the path to happiness even when they hurt us, forgiving them because "they know not what they do," helping them where we can, but never allowing ourselves to be bound by the quality of THEIR thought.

THROUGH THE APPARENT TO THE REAL

It means the cultivating of our ability to pierce the veil of the material with all its seeming reality, and to penetrate to the inner hidden world of true Reality, where all things have their origin, and whence all things emerge into the seen world. It means absorption in the contemplation of Omniscience, Omnipotence, and Omnipresence, with all their underlying principles, and knowing that therein lies the true world of causation. It means concentrating on causes rather than effects, knowing that effects will assuredly come once the proper causes are set in motion. It is a movement from the outer side of life to the inner.

This is why we constantly stress the fact that we treat the thought rather than the condition. The TRUE healing is the healing of the thought; the outward healing is this healed thought shadowed forth in this, our less real world of the outer.

In treating for prosperity, therefore, we do not treat for the ten-dollar bill; we get down to the unfailing PRINCIPLE of SUPPLY.

TREATMENT FOR SUPPLY

To return to our method: Again we start with the fact that man is in the small what God is in the large. We cannot conceive of the Infinite as ever being "short" of anything. Man believes he is short of things because he cannot or does not see the Infinite supply. We try to correct or counteract his false belief.

We stress the obvious fact that SUPPLY has been constant from his birth, although the CHANNELS through which it has come have been many and varied. Starting with the infant's milk, he has had three meals a day until now, and he has been clothed and housed. That supply has come through temporary channels, such as his mother, his father, odd jobs in boyhood, steady jobs in manhood. In the latter case, some of the companies from which he drew his supply may have gone out of business, or he may, voluntarily, have left their employ. But no matter for what reason, those channels were temporary.

The only changeless thing in this man's whole picture has been SUPPLY. He may have thought that the company was supplying him, because it gave him a pay check; but it was only the temporary channel through which this never ceasing supply was finding its way to him. Since it has been continuous in the past, he can logically expect it to be continuous in the future.

There has been no stoppage of supply for the Infinite; there has been no stoppage for him. There will be no stoppage for the Infinite; there will be none for him. "Shall not your Father clothe you, O ye of little faith?" (Matt. 6:30)

Here is the crux: Man's supply never fails from the other side; but, because of his little faith, he pinches it into a tiny trickle. He has developed false beliefs in obstruction and delay, and in the difficulty of the Infinite Mind's turning invisible supply into visible substance. It is no more difficult for Mind to make gold than to make sand or grass, but OUR BELIEF MAKES IT DIFFICULT.

SAMPLE TREATMENT FOR SUPPLY

I know that John Smith, of 1111 Manchester Road, Townville, is in the small that which the Infinite is in the large. He is forever in touch with an Infinite Supply, of which there can never be any shortage or depletion.

His false belief has turned his mind toward channels instead of toward the reservoir. He has allowed his fears to clog up his channels. He has had his mind on the particular, rather than on the general; on channels, rather than on the fact that supply is never-failing; on things, rather than on principles.

In this moment, I turn away from his financial needs, debts, obligations, where his thought has so long lingered. I turn to the great, unchanging Principle of Supply; I seek for him the inner Kingdom of God. I see him united with a never-ceasing flow of good, which takes the form of that which he needs in his outer affairs.

I speak my word, knowing that his consciousness is now wide open to the resources of the Infinite, and that there is nothing in his belief that hinders their flow through him. Opportunities are now presenting themselves to him, doors are opening to him as his consciousness awakens, people are seeing his true worth, and he is amply and adequately compensated for whatever effort he puts forth.

Supply flows through his consciousness easily, freely, copiously, continuously, and effortlessly, and manifests itself in his outer affairs.

I release this word to that Infinite Servant which Jesus directed to turn water into wine, feed the five thousand, heal the sick, and which pours supply this day into two billion earth dwellers, as well as feeding the countless trillions of lower forms of life from Its inexhaustible resources. It controls a million worlds in space, easily and effortlessly. John Smith's fullest, most copious supply is infinitesimal to it; therefore, I give thanks for it, even BEFORE John Smith and I see it in form, because IT IS SO.

AN ANALYSIS OF THE ABOVE
TREATMENT FOR SUPPLY

The student will notice that we have used the idea of his TRUE WORTH and VALUE being recognized. Very often the person in need thinks only of what he wants, instead of what he has to give. No one helps us out of our poverty just because he likes to do so. Our treatment for John Smith is partially a treatment of prospective employers and customers, who will see the worth of John's goods or his services, and want to avail themselves of them.

The treatment also helps correct John's faulty view, turning it from wanting to giving. Every contract must be equally valuable to the two parties. It is not enough to take pity on John and give him a job. John must have something that is valuable to that employer, or his bargain is unfair. Moreover, John must himself be conscious of his true worth if others are to come into that same consciousness.

John's trouble is not LACK, but a belief in his worthlessness. He may strenuously deny this, saying that he is a better worker than nine-tenths of those employed; but somewhere in his DEEPER mind there is always some sense of insufficiency, either unrecognized or unadmitted, which keeps him from richly paid employment. The student must treat this false belief, or John will lose the next job he gets or the next money he saves.

Few uninstructed persons know the extreme complexity of their DEEPER minds, and seldom dream of the real causes of their difficulties. The student must do it for them, and treat them accordingly.

HOW TO TREAT COLDS

In treating colds and similar ailments, it is necessary to know that the wet feet or the draught is only the exciting cause of the trouble. The underlying, predisposing cause is confusion, usually accompanied by strong feelings of inner rage and frustration.

This is supported by thousands of tests made in hospitals and clinics. It has been found that the above-mentioned causes are often tied in with the love life or with situations involving the emotions particularly.

The treatment, then, is not to know that the cold will leave, but that this particular person is coming into a new experience of peace and fulfillment.

In all treatments, the idea of peace, serenity, and tranquility should be included, because in all conditions requiring healing, including the physical and financial, these three states of mind will be found to be absent; therefore, the manifestation of peace in the patient would mean that his trouble has gone.

SUMMARY

By this time the student is coming to see that treatment is not just the waving of a magic wand while he utters a lot of hocus-pocus; it requires intelligent thought and clear reasoning, and it involves more than just ridding himself of his current misery. Treatment effects fundamental changes in his way of looking at life.

It has been noticed that when a person is healed through the spiritual method of the SCIENCE OF MIND, HIS WHOLE OUTLOOK ON LIFE is bettered. He becomes a kindlier, more tolerant, more unselfish person who no longer demands that everything shall revolve about him and his wishes. He begins to meet life as it comes with an ability to adjust himself to it — the sign of an emotionally mature, well-balanced individual. His THOUGHT as well as his body is healed. Of the two, the healing of his thought is more important. Thus, the whole man is healed.

These sample treatments have been given so that the student may use them as guides to work out his own individual treatments for particular conditions of diverse nature.

SPECIAL HELPS IN STUDYING THE LESSON

These study-helps have been carefully prepared to help you get the most out of this course.

QUESTIONS

Educators have found that a series of questions enables the student to get a complete picture of the material studied. You will find the questions accompanying each lesson highly valuable in uncovering concepts which you might otherwise pass by.

We advise that you first study the lesson carefully, then put it aside, write the answers to the questions, and, finally, *check your answers by the lesson.*

Keep the answers as a running commentary on the course *for your own benefit.* At its conclusion you will find that they have become a record of your own growth in consciousness.

1. Where does irritation originate?
2. What other conditions can you name which could also be healed by a treatment for peace?
3. List at least five practical points in treatment.
4. What is the fundamental difference between the material approach to supply and the spiritual approach shown in Jesus' teaching?
5. Explain the difference between the *Source* and the *channel.*

WRITING SUGGESTION

Write a treatment for health for yourself or another using either method.

READING SUGGESTIONS

It is not imperative that the student read the books suggested for collateral reading, but we strongly recommend that he do so for deeper insight into the subjects treated.

The books suggested may be available in your public library. If not, they may be purchased from our Book Department. Please consult our *Book Catalogue.*

Frederick Bailes, *Your Mind Can Heal You,* Ch. IX
Basil King, *The Conquest of Fear,* Ch. VI
Robert A. Russell, *You Too Can Be Prosperous*
Ralph Waldo Trine, *In Tune with the Infinite,* Chs. IV & IX
Margery Wilson, *Your Personality and God,* Ch. XII

THOUGHT-TRAINING FOR THE WEEK

Practice seeing back of the visible manifestation of the good things of life the invisible Infinite Source.

A DAILY THOUGHT

Let this thought be your daily thought during the week that you study this lesson:

Infinite Intelligence has a passion for healing; therefore, the Father wants me to manifest this good as much as I do.

A DAILY SELF-TREATMENT
(To be spoken quietly and thoughtfully each morning and evening)

"The Lord is my Shepherd. I shall not want for any good thing. This day I dare to believe that the tree of life is loaded with all the good that I desire.

"Streams of energy flow through every section of my body. My mind is at peace. My surroundings are harmonious. I like the people with whom I live and work, and they like me.

"I am amply recompensed for all my efforts. I give of my best, and it is appreciated. I leave the completing of my good to the Shepherd, in whose presence I shall dwell forever."

SCIENCE OF MIND

Home-Study Extension Course

(copyright 1951)

by

DR. FREDERICK BAILES

LESSON X

TREATMENT FOR SPECIFIC CONDITIONS
(continued)

LOVE AND MARRIAGE

The student by now can readily understand why the body can be healed through spiritual treatment. He has also come to see how his inward negative attitudes may be changed sufficiently for him to draw prosperity into his life. Now we shall see how, through spiritual means, he may draw a life partner.

Man can draw into his life anything that he wishes—IN REASON. Lest this last phrase suggest that we are placing a limitation on the Law, we shall explain by saying that we do not think that anyone could grow a green skin on his body because he happens to like that color. But he can bring into his life anything for his growth and happiness, and love and marriage certainly are in this category. Time after time we have seen somewhat plain, unattractive persons, both men and women, draw a greatly enriching love into their lives after they have grasped the underlying principle by which this is brought about.

Before we go into the way in which this may be done, we should say that it is precisely the same method by which one draws any good thing into his life: the right employment, the right place to live, customers to one's business, or sales from one's calls. This course stresses PRINCIPLES, because the fundamental PRINCIPLE, once grasped, can be applied at a great number of points.

We shall now apply the principle to love and marriage and, later in the lesson, to other aspects of one's life.

The Reasoning Method of treatment has usually been found best for this purpose, because the seeker very often has to reverse his past ways of looking at the problem, and build an entirely new type of consciousness to attain his end.

WHAT DO I HAVE TO GIVE IN MARRIAGE?

In the first place, the seeker for marital happiness must turn away from what he or she wants, and approach the situation from the standpoint of what he or she has to offer which will bring completion to the life of another. The person who is seeking a marriage partner should make a list on paper of all his or her abilities and qualities that might appeal to the type of partner desired. The following questions are suggestions for doing this:

Am I home-loving, or career-minded, or travel-minded? Is my disposition good? Can I refrain from snapping back if something is said to displease me? Am I usually cheerful? Do I submerge my wishes to a reasonable extent, or do I always insist on having my own way? Do I keep myself well-groomed? Am I extravagant or miserly? Am I gossipy?

Am I warm and affectionate? Do I have initiative? the ability to make decisions? Am I suspicious or jealous? Am I flirtatious? What subjects am I able to discuss reasonably well? What talents and skills have I? In what stratum of society could I be a worthy part?

WE MUST GIVE HAPPINESS
IN ORDER TO RECEIVE IT

We must agree with Emerson that no one has the right to anything that is not his by right of consciousness. By this we mean that there is a certain level at which we can fulfill the life of another. Quite naturally we do not wish to marry below this level, for then the other person could never bring us real happiness. On the other hand, we have no right to expect this Law to bring us someone so much above our level that our presence would be a constant source of embarrassment or disappointment to him or her. We might be perfectly happy to have HIM—and we are using the pronoun as the common gender—but we might be robbing him of happiness if he should have US. This would be imbalance; the Law is a law of balance.

Any contract to be fair must equally benefit both parties. Each must willingly continue in it. Each must permanently feel, "I'm glad that I found you, of all the people in the world." This is the only basis for a happy marriage.

An illiterate woman might be supremely happy with a college professor, but her constant grammatical blunders might make him ashamed of her. A rough, tough, cursing stevedore might be proudly happy with a refined, sheltered little Dresden china lady, but his every gesture might be an affront to her.

We have a right to draw to us only that which harmonizes with us, and to be drawn only to that person with whom we are well harmonized. Perhaps the best way of putting it would be this: we should treat to draw to us that person whom we enjoy as he is, and whom we have no desire to change; and that person must like us as we are, and have no desire that we be anything different from what we are.

WHAT DO I EXPECT TO RECEIVE IN MARRIAGE?

We said earlier that a treatment is a DEFINITE movement of Mind. This Law that we use is a Law of Reflection. It reflects, as a mirror, ONLY that which is placed before it. It is not enough to say, "I want to marry." The Law can project our wish into form, but WHAT we marry might be quite different from what we really want; therefore, it is well to set down on paper the type of person wanted —his or her qualities, special interests, likes and dislikes, accomplishments in general, and, if a man, his earning power. Do not put down trivialities but only those things which are necessary to perfect harmony. If it doesn't matter whether he is tall or short, or she is blonde or brunette, leave it out.

Divorce judges tell us that the three most common obstacles to happy marriage are drinking, gambling, and infidelity. The mere presence of the first two are not necessarily barriers, provided they are not carried to excess. Many fine people like a cocktail or like to spend a day at the races or an evening at poker; but when these are carried to excess, which is destructive, they can break up a marriage. Some spouses like to join the partner in a moderate amount of these diversions; but if the one seeking a mate is a violent teetotaler or a non-gambler, the treatment should specify that one is attracting a mate not given to these habits at all. There is no question but that infidelity will break up a marriage; so this must be included in the "non-wanted's."

Sometimes a man has previous ties. He may be living apart or with his wife, who, he says, "doesn't understand" him. Know now that this sort of love affair is a dead-end street.

Another tie that may bind either a man or a woman is children by a former marriage. A person may be so much a slave to the children that a spouse must always take second place. This is a frequent cause of marital unhappiness. Normal, balanced ties with the children are admirable, and if the new spouse can establish warm relationships with the children, the marriage is strengthened; if the children resent the new partner, the marriage can be destroyed.

A third tie which should be considered is inordinate subjection to a parent. Sometimes a mother—or, in rarer cases, a father—has kept the child so tied to the apron strings that the parent comes before the spouse.

On our paper, therefore, should be a statement to the effect that "there are no previous ties which take precedence over ours."

To sum it up, the two lists which we have made should include all those essentials for a happy and balanced marriage with emphasis on these: one person with the ability to provide for the upkeep of the home, the other with the ability to make that home a real home, both with dispositions and mental levels that harmonize with each other.

WHAT YOU ARE SEEKING IS SEEKING YOU

The next paragraph, which touches on fundamentals taken up in previous lessons, may seem at first glance to have no place just here; but since they have to do with the "why" and "how" of manifestations, it is well that the seeker be reminded of them at this point. Their application to companionship in marriage will follow.

The student, advanced this far, knows that everything — past, present, and future — is now floating in that stream of consciousness which we call Infinite Mind. We do not so much originate thought as we register thought which already is in the Infinite Mind. All future inventions are already known in that Mind long before human "inventors" grope their uncertain way toward them. When a man "invents," or a scientist makes a new "discovery," it merely means that these persons are sensitive enough in that department of their thinking to register ideas which are carried along in the river of Mind.

Now to get back to our seeker for a mate who asks, "Why have I desired this particular sort of person whose description I have put down on paper?" The answer is, "Because someone, somewhere, of exactly this type is wishing that he (common gender) could meet someone just like me. He is not attracted to those in his immediate environment, and wishes that a person of my appearance and personality might come his way. Then he would marry."

NO COMPETITION FOR LOVE

This does not mean, if you are a woman, that you are more beautiful, or younger, or more mature or, if you are a man, that you are a better provider, than others. It simply means that the tie which binds two together is like an invisible thread running through you and this type of person. The fact that you are attracted to a person having the qualities that you have outlined indicates that you, likewise, are intuitively in harmony with that sort of person; therefore, others of a different type leave you cold. Your picture of the ideal is, then, your response to his call, and his picture of his ideal is his answer to your desire.

The Infinite Mind is ceaselessly separating that which is not in harmony, and drawing together that which is in harmony. This is the lesson of chemistry, biology, and all the other sciences. It is true also in the mental and spiritual fields. The word "affinity" has been degraded to the position of an illicit relationship, but in its noblest sense there are affinities which make for the perfect marriage. They are the result of the intelligent approach to this problem, made through the SCIENCE OF MIND, by two individuals who understand the principle.

The future mate may be thousands of miles away at this moment. That does not matter. Omnipresence knows exactly where he (she) is, and when properly approached, will bring the two together. The seeker's province is that of keeping this thought clear and decisive on this point. IT IS THE FUNCTION OF INFINITE CREATIVE MIND TO OPEN THE CHANNELS AND PROVIDE THE MEANS.

One of the things this SCIENCE OF MIND approach does is to remove all sense of competition. We are never in competition with anyone whom we might consider having more appeal than we have. One has only to look about at his friends to know that beauty, without a doubt, must be "in the eye of the beholder." There must be some invisible bond holding many couples together, because nothing on the exterior could account for some unions; yet they are highly satisfactory.

There IS someone who will see us as the ideal, and whom we shall see as the ideal. And there is NO competition.

We are going to repeat something that we said earlier: one of the fundamental reasons why the good we long for does not come to us is because, as soon as we desire it, we immediately begin to think up all the reasons why it can NOT come true. This negative attitude effectually blocks the channels through which our good might come to us. Now, in our new attitude, we shall cultivate the habit of thinking of all the reasons why it CAN come true. Those negative reasons, which are so easy to find, we quickly place in the background and forget. We CHOOSE to draw into the foreground only the positive reasons why our desire CAN come to pass. This is highly important, for nothing in the universe denies us our good BUT WE OURSELVES.

The woman seeking a mate must also break away from the general thought of those who negatively discuss such matters. How often do we hear, "There are three women to every man," or "Men of my (middle) age want young girls." While these statements are true ONLY to those who believe them, a lie believed will act as if it were the truth. As long as a woman parrots these statements, she is holding her good away from her. To bolster step five in treatment, which is reasoning, read the vital statistics column in the papers and see how many women of your years appear there. This will help remove this false barrier.

TREATMENT FOR THOSE SEEKING A MATE

The treatment should be somewhat as follows:

I know that I am an extension of Infinite Mind; therefore, what is true of It is also true of me. It is never separated from Its good, nor does It ever experience any incompleteness at any point in Its experience.

My incompleteness has been a false experience, growing out of my false belief about myself and about life. I now reverse my belief, and this word is the expression of my new belief.

I am fully conscious of my own true worth, and those I meet are likewise conscious of it. I know that somewhere there is someone who needs and wants me as much as I do him (her) and who will never be fully contented in life until I become a part of the completed circle. He (she) needs me to make a completely rounded life.

This person is thus and so (enumerating the qualities on the paper) and hungers for someone with these qualities (your own on the paper). Our coming together will be the richest fulfillment of life for both of us, for each likes and enjoys the other just as he (she) is.

The Infinite Mind knows where each is, and is even now moving beneath the surface to bring us together. I leave it entirely to the Infinite, knowing that at this moment the hidden currents of Its activity are in motion to this end. Thus I release my word completely to that Mind which unites those who are attuned to each other. It knows the ways and means. I know that It has brought together every happy couple who have ever been united, that It has every eligible person in Its thought, and that my quiet expectation is the signal for It to move into action. It knows only completeness; therefore, It is completing two lives by making them one. And IT IS SO.

- 7 -

The question arises, "Is it right to treat that a certain person will fall in love with us?"

In the SCIENCE OF MIND we do not do this because it savors of coercion and hynotism. It is to be remembered that we do not fall in love with a person so much as with a type. We have referred to the fact that there seems to be an invisible thread running through life which draws certain TYPES of persons toward each other. Any happily married person could have married any one of ten thousand individuals, and would have been just as happy. But those ten thousand would have had the same hidden something that is the basis of true, mutual appeal. For example, if we had lived in Finland, we never would have met the present partner, but could have been equally happy with one of the right type found there.

OUR PART FOLLOWING TREATMENT

Our treatment, therefore, leaves to Infinite Mind the bringing to us of the particular individual. Since happiness in marriage must be equal on both sides, Infinite Mind does not specialize on a particular person we might select, because, as we said before, while we might be very happy with him, he might have good reasons for not finding happiness with us.

This does not mean that we must be recessive, nor does it prevent our making ourselves attractive to a particular person. We may be as attractive as we can, provided we are not putting on a veneer. But it is well to remember that it is sincerity and not tricks, that has the greatest appeal, whether it be in woman or in man.

To the woman who works where all the men are married, or who teaches school, or who says, "I never go anywhere where I meet eligible men," we say that these seeming barriers are no barriers to Infinite Mind. And since it is the work of Infinite Mind, and not herself, to bring together that which is in harmony, there is no reason why she should not meet eligible men ANYWHERE she goes, or at any gathering that she attends. Let her cultivate an INNER sense of quiet expectancy. BUT NEVER, NEVER LET UNDUE EAGERNESS SHOW IN HER MANNER.

We could have devoted all this space to relating many cases in our files of people who have happily married long after they had given up hope of doing so; however, we felt it would be of more benefit to the student to outline the METHOD by which these persons were helped to rearrange their thoughts, and thus draw their happiness to them. But NO one is too unbeautiful, or too old, or too unattractive externally to draw his (her) mate, unless he (she) holds a fixed belief along these lines.

SALESMANSHIP

The principle here for the salesman is that a sale must not be just something that HE wants. His prospect must want to buy or to be shown that it is to his advantage to buy, and he must be equally satisfied after he has bought. True, the salesman works because he wants the commission, but until he SEES HIS SALE AS A SERVICE TO THE OTHER FELLOW, he will not be a GREAT salesman nor a scientific salesman.

He must treat to know that there are thousands upon thousands of persons, not satisfied with what they now have, who want and are ready to buy the goods that he has to sell. They may never have heard of his merchandise or services, but they have an unrecognized hunger for them; and when the salesman presents his goods to them, something within them will make them glad to get what he has to offer.

RIGHT HOUSING

Whether there is a housing shortage or not, every person wants the right place to live. The seeker for right housing can know this: that there IS a house or an apartment that has never been properly lived in until he lives in it; that the owner either knowingly or unknowingly wants his type of person for a tenant; that the locality is just what he likes; the price is within his financial range; the neighbors are easy to live with; the rooms are arranged to suit his purpose; and any other detail that he thinks necessary.

Infinite Mind knows where that place is, and when we release our desire to it, a movement starts within MIND to open up the channels for the bringing together of place and tenant.

As we have stressed before, we stress again, that the important thing for the student to grasp is the PRINCIPLE. The applications of the principle are many. We might liken it to a vacuum cleaner which works according to a certain principle of electricity, and to which many kinds of attachments can be adjusted. Once a person knows how to plug it in and turn the switch, it is simply a matter of choice as to which attachment he will use.

SECURING NEEDED CAPITAL

To the person who may need capital for his business, we say— let him start to build the inward conviction that somewhere there is an individual who lives from investments and who wishes he knew where there is a sound place to invest his money.

Many persons who were either starting or expanding their business have come to us for treatment along this line, persons who for months had unsuccessfully knocked on doors and butted their heads against brick walls trying to raise the necessary capital. Once they had learned the truly scientific way of arranging their thought-life, they found doors to capital swinging open, often before they had knocked.

DRINKING AND OTHER DESTRUCTIVE HABITS

It is now well established that excessive drinking is an emotional rather than a physical illness. It invariably springs from a conscious or unconscious sense of inadequacy at one or more points in the life. The drinker is first a person with a sense of defeat who is running away from his recognition of his insufficiency somewhere, although he might be quite successful financially.

Man was created for winning, not losing. When he wins, he is in tune with life and with the Source of life. He loves to succeed and hates to fail. All the generations of overcomers from which he has descended speak to him in his blood, brain, and nervous system. Man is of noble ancestry, therefore cannot stand the humiliation which failure brings. Even the little child undergoes painful feelings of shame and humiliation when scolded or scorned. Men have waited years to kill someone who has humiliated them. The expression "I was so mortified I could have DIED" is truer than appears.

Drinking raises one's ego. After a few drinks the mousy man, who has always failed to assert himself, becomes noisy and quarrelsome, and sometimes tries to take the officer's club away from him. He may become boastful, relating as true experiences that which is only dreamy fantasy. Thus alcohol takes away the bitter awareness of failure, making him a "king for a day" in a make-believe sense. He may play God by giving money away.

More drinks carry him beyond this stage of false self-sufficiency into one in which his sense of failure will not down. Sober, he would be ashamed to be seen crying, but now, with his inhibitions removed, he moves into a "crying jag," in which his DEEPER MIND unashamedly admits what he has consciously avoided recognizing—his failure. In this stage he sometimes talks of taking his life, which supports our statements in the second paragraph under the above heading.

This death wish is carried out vicariously in the terminal stage of drinking, in which he "passes out." Further drinking has carried him past the stage of boasting, self-pity, crying, shame. He loses interest in his surroundings and sinks slowly into oblivion, the temporary equivalent of death. But the entire cycle has been negative, starting with a sense of defeat and ending in a complete running away from it. Nothing has been solved.

TREATING THE EXCESSIVE DRINKER

If one's mind can be elevated to the consciousness of power and self-sufficiency under the influence of alcohol, a narcotic, it shows that it can be raised to that same level WITHOUT the narcotic, for drugs do not create power; they merely uncover powers that already are a part of one's mental make-up. Alcohol provided *pictures* of self-sufficiency. The mind has other material capable of producing the same pictures of adequacy without alcohol.

Our previous lessons showed that man is in the small what God is in the large, that all of the Infinite adequacy is in man, and that when he cultivates a sense of oneness with the Infinite, the nature and powers of the Infinite flow through him. It is a striking fact that there is seldom a true deliverance from excessive drinking unless this union of God and man is stressed. No one ever defeats alcohol by gritting his teeth and fighting furiously against it. He whips it by turning TOWARD something more potent and more desirable. A treatment that has proved efficacious follows:

Harry Jones is a part of that Infinite Person whose roots are in eternity; he partakes of the divine nature, which has never been blocked nor defeated at any point in its experience. He is completely adequate to meet life at any point, without any false stimulation. He is now a "God-intoxicated person," filled with a sense of unbreakable oneness with the Infinite. God's thoughts are his thoughts; there is no room for failure thoughts, for he is one with all the currents of life. He does not have to fight liquor; he simply does not respond to its appeal; his desire for it has vanished in his new-found oneness with Infinite Wisdom and Power. He is dead to it because he is alive to the Christ in him. Life has a new meaning for him—he penetrates deeper into the heart and reality of things; he is united with all that contains beauty and is mentally and emotionally separated from everything that is ugly or destructive. Life has purpose for him— he sees it stretching ahead, leading him into self-fulfillment, usefulness, and satisfactory achievement.

I speak my word for Harry Jones, knowing that the galleries of his mind are filled with pictures of those things which are "lovely, noble, pure, and of good report" and that it is not he, but the Father within him, that doeth the work. This is my highest thought for Harry Jones and I release it completely to the Infinite Mind, knowing as I do, that it IS so."

SUMMARY

Never forget that the Infinite Mind is the Knower. It knows where all persons, places, and things which are in harmony with one another are. It would always bring them together were it not for man's ignorance. Man blocks the channels by which his good might come to him by building mental pictures of the extreme difficulty of raising money or finding a place to live, or getting the right job, or selling enough customers.

Man needs to know that he has a Silent Partner, who is a better real estate agent than the best human living, a more intelligent capital raiser than the best promoter, a better physician than the most skillful doctor, a better intermediary than the most successful marriage broker. This Partner is always ready to bring things to completion. The only thing that can stop this Partner from doing so is man's own obstructive thought.

This Knower is the Opener of the gates, the Dissolver of problems. Nothing is too insignificant for Its attention, nothing too hard for Its power, nothing too intricate for Its skill. Every second of every hour It works, ceaselessly weaving the pattern of our thoughts into the pattern of our affairs. But It can work only with the threads of thought WE give It.

Therefore, our business is not to sit despondently WISHING or praying that our negative conditions will change, but to select positive, constructive threads of thought, release them to Infinite Mind, then leave the rest to the ONE CREATIVE AGENCY that can bring about a conclusion that is satisfactory and fair to everyone concerned.

SPECIAL HELPS IN STUDYING THE LESSON

These study-helps have been carefully prepared to help you get the most out of this course.

LESSON X

QUESTIONS

Educators have found that a series of questions enables the student to get a complete picture of the material studied. You will find the questions accompanying each lesson highly valuable in uncovering concepts which you might otherwise pass by.

We advise that you first study the lesson carefully, then put it aside, write the answers to the questions, and, finally, *check your answers by the lesson.*

Keep the answers as a running commentary on the course *for your own benefit.* At its conclusion you will find that they have become a record of your own growth in consciousness.

1. Explain Emerson's statement that no one has the right to anything that is not his by right of consciousness.
2. Why should we be definite in what we expect of another in marriage?
3. Why do we decide not on a certain person but on a person with certain qualities?
4. How must a salesman consider his sale in relation to the buyer?

WRITING SUGGESTION

Write a treatment for love and marriage, a home, the business, or any personal desire other than health, using either method.

READING SUGGESTIONS

It is not imperative that the student read the books suggested for collateral reading, but we strongly recommend that he do so for deeper insight into the subjects treated.

The books suggested may be available in your public library. If not, they may be purchased from our Book Department. Please consult our *Book Catalogue.*

Frederick Bailes, "Getting Along with Troublesome People" and "Getting What You Go After"

Kahlil Gibran, *The Prophet,* "On Love," "On Marriage," "On Giving," "On Buying and Selling"

THOUGHT-TRAINING FOR THE WEEK

Practice giving of your thought this week. Give on the mental level by kindly words to others and considerate attention to what they are saying. Give on the spiritual level by good thoughts about them either in specific treatment or in casual thought.

A DAILY THOUGHT

Let this thought be your daily thought during the week that you study this lesson:

Every moment the Infinite Mind is drawing together those persons, places, and things that are in harmony with each other, and separating those that are not in harmony.

A DAILY SELF-TREATMENT

(To be spoken quietly and thoughtfully each morning and evening)
"I understand that I am one with all the constructive forces in the universe, and that all the harmonious currents of life are drawn to me and operate through me. I have established a right relation to Divine Mind.

"I am surrounded by perfect understanding this day as I make contacts with other persons. All my domestic, social, and occupational relationships are marked by the Divine harmony and understanding. I have mentally established a right relation to others. My body experiences harmony within itself and with the surrounding cells."

SCIENCE OF MIND

Home-Study Extension Course

(copyright 1951)

by

DR. FREDERICK BAILES

LESSON XI

PRACTICAL POINTS IN TREATMENT

In this lesson we shall discuss several points in treatment which we have found effective during the more than quarter of a century that we have helped to perfect the SCIENCE OF MIND method of dealing with life. There will be moments in the student's healing work when his treatment seems to be getting nowhere, and it is then that he will find invaluable the dramatization of some enlightening point which may occur to him in treatment and which will break the mental block that has delayed the healing.

QUALITY AND QUANTITY OF BELIEF

Before we take up these methods, however, it is well to emphasize the fact that to heal any condition, whether it relates to health, finance, employment, marital happiness, or any other state, it is imperative that the student turn away from the false to concentrate his focus of attention on the correct belief. Whether a healing is gradual or instantaneous depends entirely on the speed with which the one who treats can substitute the new viewpoint for the old.

INSTANTANEOUS HEALING

During our Sunday morning services, where a high state of consciousness is attained by the thousands who attend, healings are frequently instantaneous. Scarcely a service passes but that someone

- 1 -

approaches the speaker to say something like this: "This is my first Sunday here, and a persistent headache or body pain that I have had for weeks completely disappeared while you were speaking. Could it actually be cured in such a short time?"

The answer is that the greatest Authority on this Law once said, "It is done unto you AS ye believe." "As" refers to quality and quantity. It means THE WAY we believe. When the conviction of the Power outweighs the fear of the condition, both the quality and quantity of the belief are satisfactory and the healing occurs. Moreover, it can happen in the twinkling of an eye. These are called instantaneous healings.

Men who have not drawn a sober breath nor earned an honest dollar in years have staggered into rescue missions and have had the whole course of their lives changed in a few minutes' time. Somehow, a single illuminating thought has penetrated the alcoholic mists be-clouding their minds and so changed the focus of their belief that they have become useful and respected citizens. This changed belief has been brought about in a few minutes' time.

It is by this change of focus that healing occurs in the SCIENCE OF MIND method. Actually there are no healers, as such. The one giving a treatment does not heal the person he treats. But he does change his own false belief about that person's condition, and in so doing tunes in on the Principle, to which all have access and which accomplishes the healing.

QUALITIES OF THE GOOD PRACTITIONER

We have stressed the fact, that in metaphysical treatment, there are two extremes which are to be avoided: one is self-depreciation; the other, self-aggrandizement; and either will prevent satisfactory results.

Self-depreciation can grow out of one's fear that he has not suffi-cient education. Some of the most successful practitioners have had a limited formal education, but their consciousness of the Power of the Infinite is very strong. Some of high scholastic attainments, on the other hand, fail in treatment because of a weak healing consciousness.

Anyone who constantly thinks, "I am not good enough," will be unable to get satisfactory results. This is not because of their lack of "goodness," but because of their belief about this real or supposed lack. If goodness were a prerequisite, there would be little healing, since none of us has lived consistently on as high a level as he would desire. However, Truth unchecked can operate surprisingly through very imperfect channels; for it is the Truth, not the agent, which sets the person free. The Power is in the Healing Presence; the practitioner is only the channel through which It operates.

At the other extreme is he who thinks or speaks of himself as a "good healer." True, he may see excellent results coming from his treatment, but he is mistaken in thinking that it is himself who heals. One is not a good "illumination" because he turns on a switch. It is the law of electricity that banishes the darkness by bringing the light.

The moment we interpose anything between the Power and the patient, it becomes a hindrance. The belief in either our "goodness" or "badness" can obstruct; in fact, anything that distracts our attention from the real healing agent can become a barrier. The one who treats successfully remains humble; yet he is supremely confident of the Power by which the healing is accomplished. This is a fine point that should be well established in the student's mind. The greatest Practitioner who ever lived said, "Of myself, I can do nothing." This was his HUMILITY; but it was his CONFIDENCE that added, "The Father in me, He it is that doeth the works."

THE "DISSOLVING" METHOD

The writer was once treating a woman for the removal of a serious condition. Every few days she would telephone to report that she was no better. It was one of those stubborn cases that one sometimes encounters where, despite the best efforts of the practitioner, no improvement shows. The Analytical Method quite evidently had failed to uncover the blockage in thought; yet the one who treated knew that there were no incurable diseases, and that somewhere there must be an answer to the problem.

At home, after a busy day at the office, he sometimes relaxed before dinner by watching the slow, easy movements of the tropical fish in a large rectangular aquarium. On this particular evening, in reaching under water to move a piece of coral on the bottom, he noticed a crystal-clear streak follow where his hand had touched the glass side of the tank as he withdrew it.

The light shining through the water had given the impression that the tank was clean. But now he saw that there was a film of algae on the glass; and faced with the task of removing water, plants, and fish in order to clean the aquarium, he found himself wishing that there were some harmless solvent that could be sprinkled on the surface and that would melt away all film and dirt as it slowly sank to the bottom.

It was in that instant that the thought flashed into his mind: "This is exactly what is needed in this woman's stubborn case. You have been trying to analyze and wash away the 'film' without result. Why not sit back, relax, and watch the Infinite Healing Solvent move slowly through every cell of her body, neutralizing each last remnant of her disordered thought?"

A day or two later came the call reporting great improvement, and in a short while the condition had disappeared completely. This is not to deny the efficacy of the Analytical Method; but when one way seems not to bring good results, one may switch to another, such as the DISSOLVING treatment, with success.

THE "REFUSAL" METHOD

One day a man came to the office with an ugly looking rash that had broken out all over his body. He said that even after several months of medication, diet, etc., dermatologists had been unable to help him; and he added, "This thing has got me down. I'm really afraid. I try to keep my thoughts right, but even in my most hopeful moments, it persists."

Our answer was, "Suppose a man came to your door right now with an elephant. Suppose he told you he was disbanding his circus, and had decided to give you this tremendous beast. You reply that you do not want the animal, but he insists that he is leaving it with you just the same. You then tell the man that you have not solicited this doubtful gift, nor have you any place to house it, and if he persists in the matter, you have the right to do the final thing and say, 'I refuse to accept or to take delivery of this thing you offer.' Whereupon, you may close the door in his face, and under the law he is compelled to take the unwelcome beast away."

Precisely the same thing can be done with an unwanted condition. While it is true that we treat the thought rather than the thing, there are times when we must be very positive in regard to the thing, and we can be sure that in so doing, we are backed up by mental law.

We may say, "I did not consciously ask for this condition, nor will I accept it. It is not a part of me. No place in my body was provided to house such a thing; therefore, I refuse it. I shut the door of my consciousness in its face, for I know that 'To them that receive HIM, he gives power to become [in their bodies also] the sons of God.'" (John 1:12)

The man caught the idea. Within twenty-four hours his trouble had disappeared, for, having freed himself of the elephantine fear of the condition, the Power had an opportunity to do its work and the healing was accomplished.

THE "ESCALATOR" METHOD

The manner in which Impersonal Law can take us to any one of many diverse manifestations is exemplified by the department store escalator. All day long person after person steps onto it on his way to the department where he will find the merchandise he wants. The escalator is unaware of what they seek, and moves only in a prescribed direction that will carry ANYONE to the level he determines.

In this proceeding, however, the person must first exercise selection in deciding on what level he will find the goods he seeks. He must also use initiative, taking the necessary steps to place his feet on the moving stairs. The escalator will not reach out and drag him aboard, nor will it wait a single instant; it just keeps moving upward. Once the person steps aboard, however, it becomes his servant, with full responsibility to carry him to the higher level he has selected.

We outlined this escalator method to a young student who had tried repeatedly to interview a certain influential man about a job he very much desired. He had never been able to get past the man's secretary, his letters had gone unanswered, and he was discouraged and doubtful that he knew enough about the Law to make it work for him.

During our talk the young man began to see that it was not necessary for him to know how the escalator worked. The important thing was that once he had stepped aboard, it knew how to transport him to the upper floor; and presently he gave his own treatment, saying:

Infinite Mind, I want that man to give me just one interview. You know how to take me to that point. I don't care how you do it, just so long as I can talk to him. See, I am putting my foot on the escalator now! I am relying on you to bring this meeting about. I know that I don't have to struggle to reach that level. You are taking me there.

On Saturday afternoons, it had been this young man's custom to caddy at the country club; and on the following Saturday, when the man he was so anxious to meet was, for the first time, a guest at the club, our young fellow was assigned to caddy for him. The man was one of a foursome, but from time to time he chatted with his alert and personable caddy; and before the eighteen holes were played, the young man had had his longed-for interview and had landed the job.

THE "FOCAL" METHOD

One case in which there was an instantaneous healing was treated in the following manner:

The writer, in his treatment, began to think of the man he was treating as sitting alone in the center of a room in his home. He began then to think of healing rays of light that flowed downward from the molding near the room's ceiling, and upward from the molding around the floor's edge, so that there was not one spot in the room that was not flooded with the rays; and all of these rays converged upon the man, coming to a focal point in him with terrific healing power.

In order not to think of these as earthly rays of physical origin, the practitioner then declared them to be totally invisible, having the Life of Spirit, and that there was nothing in the man's consciousness or body that was able to resist their positive power. Then, as we have said, the change was brought about instantaneously, and the man was healed.

THE "REPLACEMENT" METHOD

There are times when, in the midst of other duties, the practitioner is called upon for an emergency treatment; and excellent results have often followed this method:

The practitioner begins with an image of the person being treated. Naturally this is a picture of the physical man; but soon the mind of the one who treats releases the physical impression so that it gradually recedes and disappears, and in its place he allows to emerge a perfect circle or sphere. This circle he conceives to be the image of perfection, and since there are neither features, face, nor form to intrude, he is able quickly and easily to treat impersonally with his mind stayed on the Absolute of Perfection, from which Source comes all healing.

THE "ARCHITECT" METHOD

It is true that we do not treat the physical body as such. Rather, we treat the underlying thought. But there are times when the student will find the following method valuable:

Consider the beginning of a human life, which is comprised of a male and a female cell, fused into one. At the moment of fusion are sealed up in that cell all the inherited characteristics that the emerging man will manifest. Nothing more can now be added. The Infinite sees the adult man in the cell. The man IS in the cell, all organs completed, though as yet his tissues are only ideas.

From that one cell, but eventually composed of twenty-three trillion cells, the infant will presently emerge. Infinite Intelligence will cause to evolve ONLY that which was in that primary cell. In one sense, the entire man is unfolded from that cell, where he was hidden at conception. Infinite Mind knows the mechanics of building any sort of cell, never having to stop and wonder what to do next. It needs nothing but a pattern to follow, a concept to be turned into protoplasm. It moves surely and with certainty, completing the entire structure in approximately 280 days.

Every organ in man's body is a concept held in Infinite Mind. All of God's concepts are perfect and changeless; therefore, any person believing himself to be ill is looking at himself in a manner unlike the one in which the Infinite regards him. "Man looketh on the outward appearance, but the Lord looketh on the heart [the origin]." (I Sam. 16:7)

Mind is at this moment creating untold billions of cells not only in hundreds of thousands of unborn children, but also for the repair and upkeep of all ages in all manifested bodies. It is never confused. It knows what to do and is willing and eager to do it; therefore, we turn away from the seeming incurability of any condition, knowing that it is only an outward appearance. We say, "The Intelligence that built this structure knows exactly what to do to reconstruct it. It is now rebuilding while I, the practitioner, let my thought coincide with the original thought of the Infinite. I am now looking on the cell, the spiritual concept, the original building, seeing it as perfect as does God, whose concept of its perfection has never changed."

In the treatment just outlined, we see that in reality there is nothing to heal. Our work is only to correct our tendency to look at the outer effect, thus changing our viewpoint to focus on the inner Cause, which is eternally perfect. There will be an outer change, but the practitioner is not primarily concerned with this, nor is he responsible for it, although he welcomes it as much as the patient does.

In this ARCHITECT Method of treatment, it can be clearly seen that the healing is not so much a PROCESS as it is a REVELATION of the Truth about man. Whatever process is involved belongs entirely in the province of Divine Intelligence, and consists only in the actual physical alteration of the cells to manifest their perfection.

SPECIAL HELPS IN STUDYING THE LESSON

These study-helps have been carefully prepared to help you get the most out of this course.

QUESTIONS

Educators have found that a series of questions enables the student to get a complete picture of the material studied. You will find the questions accompanying each lesson highly valuable in uncovering concepts which you might otherwise pass by.

We advise that you first study the lesson carefully, then put it aside, write the answers to the questions, and, finally, *check your answers by the lesson.*

Keep the answers as a running commentary on the course *for your own benefit.* At its conclusion you will find that they have become a record of your own growth in consciousness.

1. How is the Law of Cause and Effect like an escalator?
2. Explain: "It is done unto you *as* you believe."
3. In treatment what only do we seek to heal?
4. What does the actual healing?
5. Explain: "Healing is not a process so much as it is a revelation of the truth about man."

WRITING SUGGESTION

Write a treatment for any condition following some special method of your own.

READING SUGGESTIONS

It is not imperative that the student read the books suggested for collateral reading, but we strongly recommend that he do so for deeper insight into the subjects treated.

The books suggested may be available in your public library. If not, they may be purchased from our Book Department. Please consult our *Book Catalogue*.

Edith Armstrong, "Help Yourself"
Frederick Bailes, "The Secret of Healing"
Bessie Beihl, *The Lord Is Your Shepherd*

THOUGHT-TRAINING FOR THE WEEK

Turn your thought this week to ways of making the Infinite Healing Presence vivid to you in your treatment.

A DAILY THOUGHT

Let this be your daily thought during the week that you study this lesson:

The Infinite Healing Presence fills this room from floor to ceiling, from wall to wall, is around and within every thing and every person within it.

A DAILY SELF-TREATMENT
(To be spoken quietly and thoughtfully each morning and evening)

"This day my soul is caught up in the assurance that the Infinite is close at hand, radiant with supreme beauty, the beauty of wholeness. It is the Infinite Healing Presence, closer to me than my breath. It is formless, nameless, beyond description or explanation, yet never beyond my personal experience. It is the All in all; there is nothing that can stand before it, oppose it, or successfully block its onward sweep.

"This wholeness is so complete that it blots out all lack and all experience of anything less than the Whole. Easily and effortlessly I surrender myself this day to that which is over all and within all."

SCIENCE OF MIND

Home-Study Extension Course

(copyright 1951)

by

DR. FREDERICK BAILES

LESSON XII

THE HEALING CONSCIOUSNESS

As the student has made his way through this preliminary or basic course, it must have become evident that the art of healing consists in something more than a mere knowledge of the techniques.

He must have seen, also, that THOUGHT is paramount and that the practitioner deals WITH NOTHING ELSE. It naturally follows that our thoughts are tools which the Infinite Sculptor uses to liberate the perfect figure which lies hidden in the block of rough stone.

We have said repeatedly that THOUGHTS ARE THINGS. The practitioner is constantly trying to produce THINGS or results by the use of his thought; therefore, the quality of those things will depend upon the quality of his thought. This quality is his CONSCIOUSNESS, which we touched upon in Lesson V. If his consciousness be of a limited order, the THINGS which issue from it will be of a limited order; if it be of a high order, the manifestation will be equally high.

CONSCIOUSNESS is not easy to define, nor are the steps into a higher consciousness easy to outline. The teacher can lead the student by the hand along the pathway of METHODS; the student himself is responsible for the development of his CONSCIOUSNESS, and must take, alone, those last steps which lead him into a high consciousness.

Man's consciousness is dependent upon his concept of God. All that any of us know of God is that which we have experienced of Him. Many persons know a great deal ABOUT God, but the practitioner must KNOW GOD DIRECTLY.

CLEARING THE PATHWAY

(a) No Censoriousness

High consciousness is a high state of mind partaking of the qualities of Spirit; therefore, if one is to develop it, certain attitudes must be removed from the thought-life. The first things to go must be envy, jealousy, censoriousness, suspicion, hatred, resentment, and certain kinds of fear. We must be broad enough to know that all men are on the pathway to individual freedom, and that those who seem to be cruel or wicked are only blind. If those people would come to see more clearly the Realities of life, they would cease to be cruel or selfish or heartless; therefore, they are to be pitied, not censured.

It is not hard to forgive when one understands this. We do not hate the hunchback or the person with a clubfoot. We recognize him as one suffering from a deformity, and we are sorry for him. An ugly disposition is as truly a mental and personality deformity as those physical handicaps; therefore, we forgive.

(b) No Self-pity

It has been stated before that self-pity also must go. It is not only a hindrance; it is a sign that the student has not clearly seen that he alone draws into his life all outer experiences. If these are oppressive, the only place where they could have been fabricated is in the buried centers of his own DEEPER mind. His own thought-attitude is responsible. Nothing else has power to bring sorrow upon him.

He does not have to change others, but, positively, he must change himself. When he has done this, he will be agreeably surprised to see how others change toward him, and how he will draw less and less of the disagreeable into his life. He will never again defeat himself by feeling sorry for himself.

(c) No Negative Discussions

The practitioner will cultivate the habit of NOT discussing the frailties or meannesses of others. The Infinite does not see them; therefore, the practitioner should not see them. This will enable him to rise above those resentful feelings which hamper the work of some practitioners. It will prevent him from taking sides in domestic or legal problems brought to him.

This latter is highly necessary in a practitioner. In disputes, he should never treat that someone else will change his conduct, or that another person will do anything. He should treat that everything hidden is being uncovered, and that right action is emerging out of what looks like wrong action so that whatever is just shall come forth into manifestation. Our human judgment may err in taking sides. The Infinite never errs.

BUILDING THE CONSCIOUSNESS

There is one Perfect Consciousness in the universe—that of the Infinite. Man's consciousness rises in proportion to his union with the Infinite Consciousness. Following are some of the pathways that advanced students have trod in making their way up into the rarefied spiritual consciousness of Infinite Spirit:

(a) Recognition of Inward Impulsion

There has always been a recognition of the inward pressure of the Infinite on man. Every higher aspiration we have ever had, every noble impulse, every desire for a higher level of understanding or of living, is a clear evidence of the inward thrust of the Infinite outward.

(b) Willingness to Co-operate

There must be a willingness to respond and to co-operate with the Infinite in this process of growth and enlargement. The thought of Divine Intelligence is perfect. This selfsame image of perfection is always held deep within man by the *christos*, or KNOWER, within him. The way he responds to what life does to him will be the indicator of his response to the image of perfection.

At this stage of man's evolution, it seems impossible for him to achieve absolute perfection in his life. The aim, rather than the attainment, is the chief consideration. His very willingness to let the Absolute work Itself out through him is the key to his growth. He starts to picture to himself the characteristics of the INFINITE THINKING, and endeavors to allow these to express themselves through him, knowing that he grows through surrender to them.

(c) A Growing Awareness of Unity

There is no "otherness" in the universe. One of the basic ideas which the Infinite must evidently hold is that there is nothing but Itself in the universe. All is from God and of God. The entire universe and every tiniest part is some part of God. There can, therefore, be no real conflict between them or within them.

The belief in duality must be wiped out and replaced with a belief in unity. Here begins the fundamental state in building consciousness. We have covered this to a certain degree in a previous lesson, but it is such an important subject that it needs amplification.

Thus, since there is no "otherness," the Infinite can never see the ugly, the distorted, the failing, the inharmonious, the ill, the wretched that man's dual vision constantly sees. God is "of purer eyes than to behold evil." (Hab. 1:13) This being so, the practitioner must cultivate the habit of denying the reality of those things he treats, of closing his eyes to them as much as he can, and of seeing that what God has made is "very good." (Gen. 1:31) Negative experiences may be real in his experience, yet not ultimate Reality.

SPIRIT'S VIEW OF THE UNIVERSE

In previous lessons we have pointed out that one should not look upon the appearance, but upon the heart—the heart and core of perfection. For this reason, we should constantly remember that Spirit sees no distortion, and we must see none. Spirit sees no cancer, no debts, no quarrels. Always and forever, It sees everything as "very good." The spiritual consciousness aligns itself with the Divine viewing of the universe.

Spirit sees only Life, always in the "beauty of Holiness," which means the beauty of wholeness. Beauty is symmetry, without distortion or imbalance. Disease is imbalance. All problems are imbalance. Spirit sees all things always in one perfect equilibrium.

The practitioner cultivates the ability to deny that which seems most real to the eye of the senses, and to penetrate deeper to the true heart of the matter, which is the unchanging and unfailing continuity of the original image of perfection.

Perhaps an illustration from the world of art will, in a way, make this clearer.

THE MASTERPIECE REVEALED

Art dealers sometimes resort to a ruse to get a masterpiece out of Europe. Since governments wishing to keep certain priceless paintings in the land of their origin have forbidden their export, a crafty dealer will take such a masterpiece to a sixth-rate artist, have a mediocre picture daubed over the original, and then present it for export.

Until the system was discovered, many valuable works of art came to this country in this way. Upon arrival here, they were placed in the hands of a person who knew how to restore the original by gently rubbing with oils. With infinite care the daub was gradually rubbed away until the masterpiece stood forth once more in all its original beauty.

The practitioner must always KNOW that beneath the surface daub of sin, illness, poverty, and misery lies the original masterpiece. Thus his trained thought removes the deceptive surface and lets the original creation stand forth.

But, just as the restorer cannot create a masterpiece, but only restore it, so the practitioner cannot create perfection, but only uncover it. Before he does this, however, he must be SURE it lies beneath the surface appearance. This is spiritual thinking.

SPIRITUAL THINKING

Normal people shy away from anything that savors of sanctimoniousness, "holiness," or "otherworldliness." Many have the idea that in order to think spiritually, they must become a little peculiar. As a matter of fact, there are no more normal persons in the world than truly spiritual thinkers, for they see things in perspective. They see all outward things as real in experience, and as experiences to shun or enjoy; but they see also the unreality of everything but the eternal values.

They are not intimidated by so-called incurable diseases, knowing them to be only the daub superimposed upon the real beauty of wholeness. Neither are they caught up by the false values of the material. They recognize that money (seen) grows out of wealth (unseen). They know the frightening experiences of life to be only thought-forms which they themselves or their fellows have created. Constantly, their spiritual vision pierces the veil of the material and penetrates to the eternal Realities.

Spiritual thinkers are none the less human in their appetites and feelings, but they invest even these with the deeper beauty of the spiritual, thus enhancing their pleasures without ever being entrapped or enslaved by them. The chief aspect of this spiritual view of life is that everything is kept in its proper place, and nothing assumes undue proportions. Only thus can they keep themselves "unspotted from the world," even while walking in the world. (James 1:27) "IN the world but not OF IT."

THE FRUITS OF SPIRITUAL THINKING

Spiritual thinkers can be the instruments of healing because trouble, which is real and pressing to others, is seen by them as a chimera, which has no real existence, no real power, no real effect, and no valid ground for continued existence. They are thus able to declare its nothingness. Since disease and other miseries are basically thought, set and molded into form, spiritual thinkers know that their enlightened thought can dissolve the unwanted form, and set up a perfect thought-pattern which the Infinite Creative Mind will follow to bring the perfect form into manifestation.

We have said that the spiritually minded man is a normal and practical man. Now, there is nothing practical about bad or destructive habits, and the student of SCIENCE OF MIND will find as he progresses that such habits will drop away from him naturally and easily, not through will-power but because he loses all desire to continue what is obviously a handicap to him—but the dropping will be the EFFECT, not the CAUSE, of his spiritual advancement.

A person may never have had the faintest impulse toward crime or infidelity; he may also be free from such habits as drinking, smoking, and cursing; yet if he gives false weight and value to material appearance, he will still be an unspiritual person.

SPIRIT SEES NO DELAYS OR OBSTRUCTION

Another aspect of the thinking of Spirit is that Spirit sees no obstructions and no delays in the completion of Its plans. Man becomes a spiritual thinker when he aligns his thinking with this attitude. The average person gets a desire, sees a goal, wishes for a result; then, even as he is caught up in happy anticipation, the negative appears. Across his line of vision float menacing obstructions, doubts, and reasons why this thing he desires might NOT come true.

One characteristic difference between the earthy thinker and the spiritual thinker is this: while the former is thinking up all the reasons why a desire CANNOT come true, the latter is assembling all the reasons why it CAN come true.

Spirit lives in the eternal NOW. Man lives in a world of time and space. With Spirit, to envisage a thing is to create it. INSTANTLY, it is done. Man falsely sees his desire as something to be achieved or "demonstrated" at some later date; consequently, his thinking is unlike that of Spirit—therefore, it is unspiritual.

SPIRIT SEES THE END FROM THE BEGINNING

In an earlier lesson we said that at the moment of conception the whole man lies already in that fertilized ovum. He is not yet formed in all or any of his parts, but he is seen by Spirit as final and complete. In like manner our demonstration is seen as in final form by Spirit AT THE MOMENT WE CONCEIVE IT. Yesterday, today, and forever are as one moment to Spirit, living in the eternal NOW; for Spirit thinks not in terms of time, process, development, or manufacture; It says, "Let there be . . . and there was." (Gen. 1:3, etc.)

MIND CARRIES OUT THE CREATIVE PROCESS

Spirit leaves all process, manufacture, evolving, and development to Infinite Mind, the working side of the Trinity. This the practitioner must also learn to do, for, when he thinks of obstruction and delay, he is thinking unspiritually. He must learn to say, "Let there be, and it IS so."

- 7 -

We repeat what we stated in a previous lesson: when one's desire is born, every channel for its fulfillment is IMMEDIATELY opened. The only thing that can close those channels is our belief in obstruction and delay.

CONSCIOUSNESS OF OMNIPOTENCE—ALL POWER

To develop the consciousness in this direction, spend time contemplating the inner meaning of Omnipotence—not just a lot of power, but ALL POWER. There is no opposing, hostile power—there could not be, there cannot be. There is NO obstructing power whatever, except a false belief in obstruction.

During treatment, think up EVERY reason that this desired experience should come forth. Recall successful healings or demonstrations that you have heard about or read about. Dwell on the reasonableness of believing that Omnipotence can never be delayed. Think how, under the intelligent handling of the Omnipotent, the huge mass of suns and stars has never been able to delay its movement one second; Niagara cannot hold back from the Falls; fifty-story buildings are held close to the spinning earth by Intelligence acting as and called by the name of gravity. These are only a few of the ways in which each individual can work out his consciousness of this and other attributes of the Infinite. There are scores of other ways.

One student reported that he developed a tremendous sense of authority growing out of his awareness of Omnipotence which he acquired in this way: Quietly he thought of all the power being generated by the automobiles on the single boulevard on which his office is located—millions of horse power rolling by, easily, effortlessly, every day.

Then he thought of the power of all the cars on all the highways of the world, of all the tractors on all the farms, the steam shovels, the machinery in all the factories, the motor power of all the airplanes, the ocean liners, the steam trains, the Diesel trucks, and the surges of electric power all over the globe until he was awed by the tremendous output of power through the hands of man.

He told himself, "The imposing might of all earth's motors compared with Omnipotence is as the power of an ant compared with that of an elephant." (Of course, this analogy is weak and imperfect, because one cannot measure Omnipotence. It is beyond a trillion units of power, as represented by this comparative weighing of power as seen in ant and elephant.)

Finally, our student thought: "All this power flows through my word when I speak it for myself or for some other person. Nothing on earth CAN stop or obstruct it; nothing in heaven wishes to stop or obstruct it. It is done unto me NOW, AT THIS MOMENT, as I believe."

FINAL WORD AND BLESSING

In conclusion, we would encourage you, the student, by saying that the moment you enrolled for this course you started currents of mental and spiritual energy flowing which are continuing to operate within you whether you are conscious of them or not.

You are making greater progress than you know. People in this work always do. Sometimes they become discouraged because they constantly see loftier heights which their feet have not yet trod. The very seeing of the heights is an evidence of growth.

The spiritual person is always much more spiritual than he realizes. His discontent with his "unspirituality" is an evidence of spirituality. His desire, plus his study, sets up a spiritualizing process deep within him, and as this is not seen on the surface, he usually does not know that it is going on; but there is a constant, steady purification of the soul that surrenders to these ideas; he can depend on this.

There is a beautiful hymn sung in some churches which starts:

Take TIME to be holy;
Speak oft with thy soul.

This, the student must do. Consciousness grows wherever and whenever the student communes often with his innermost self; for in every man, as there was in Jesus, is that place where spirit with Spirit can meet. In the silences of one's thinking he comes close to God, and in that mystical meeting is communion; out of communion comes understanding; out of understanding comes power, and out of power come results.

Let us not be weary in well doing; for in due season we shall reap, if we faint not. (Gal. 6:9)

SPECIAL HELPS IN STUDYING THE LESSON

These study-helps have been carefully prepared to help you get the most out of this course.

QUESTIONS

Educators have found that a series of questions enables the student to get a complete picture of the material studied. You will find the questions accompanying each lesson highly valuable in uncovering concepts which you might otherwise pass by.

We advise that you first study the lesson carefully, then put it aside, write the answers to the questions, and, finally, *check your answers by the lesson.*

Keep the answers as a running commentary on the course *for your own benefit.* At its conclusion you will find that they have become a record of your own growth in consciousness.

1. What does a healing consciousness mean to you?
2. What does a belief in unity imply?
3. Contrast a material and a spiritual view of life.
4. How does the attitude of the unspiritually minded person differ from that of Spirit in regard to the coming forth of a demonstration?
5. What are the respective places of Spirit and of Mind in the Creative Process?

WRITING SUGGESTION

Now that you have come to the end of this course of lessons, look back over the past weeks and set down a record of your progress. In the first lesson we suggested that you list the changes that you would like to come about in your life and also the changes in thought that you should make. If you have exceeded the mark that you set for yourself, be very grateful that you have been able to do so; if you have fallen short, do not be discouraged. Good seed always grows.

READING SUGGESTIONS

It is not imperative that the student read the books suggested for collateral reading, but we strongly recommend that he do so for deeper insight into the subjects treated.

The books suggested may be available in your public library. If not, they may be purchased from our Book Department. Please consult our *Book Catalogue*.

Frederick Bailes, *Your Mind Can Heal You*, Chs. VII and X
H. B. Jeffery, *The Principles of Healing*
Ralph Waldo Trine, *In Tune with the Infinite*, Ch. X

THOUGHT-TRAINING FOR THE WEEK

As you meet in your daily associations or see as you walk down the street people who are ill or have physical malformations, or have defects of character or personality, or are undergoing some financial difficulty, practice looking right through the outer appearance to the perfect self within. In so doing you are developing your own healing consciousness and helping them at the same time.

A DAILY THOUGHT

Let this be your daily thought during the week that you study this lesson:

There is something better than being externally healed: that is, to come to know the Author of all healing.

A DAILY SELF-TREATMENT
(To be spoken quietly and thoughtfully each morning and evening)

"This day I face toward the dawn of the Infinite Healing Presence. I recognize it, like the sun coming over the hills, in an ever-growing sense of warmth, light, and life. I bathe my consciousness in its steady, serene, healing rays. I relinquish all personal struggle and effort, allowing myself to be played upon by that which is bringing healing and fulfillment. As I share the sun's rays by placing myself where they can play freely upon me, so I now place myself in the attitude of receptiveness to the Infinite Healing Presence, whose activity I welcome."

www.ingramcontent.com/pod-product-compliance
Lightning Source LLC
Chambersburg PA
CBHW080507110426
42742CB00017B/3023